A PROPHETIC VOICE IN THE CITY

Meditations on the Prophet Jeremiah

Cardinal Carlo Maria Martini
Archbishop of Milan

Translated from Italian
by
Vera Castelli Theisen

A Liturgical Press Book

THE LITURGICAL PRESS
Collegeville, Minnesota

The meditations gathered in this volume and transcribed by the recorder have not been reviewed by the author.

Cover design by Ann Blattner.

This book was originally published in Italian under the title *Una voce profetica nella città: Meditazioni sul profeta Geremia*, © 1993 by Edizioni Piemme, Casale Monferrato (AL), Italy.

The Scripture quotations are from the New Revised Standard Bible, Catholic edition, © 1989 by the Division of Christian Education of the National Council of Churches of Christ in the USA. Used by permission. All rights reserved.

1	2	3	4	5	6	7	8

Library of Congress Cataloging-in-Publication Data

Martini, Carlo Maria, 1927–
    [Voce profetica nella città.   English]
    A prophetic voice in the city : meditations on the Prophet Jeremiah / Carlo Maria Martini ; translated from Italian by Vera Castelli Theisen.
        p.   cm.
    "'A prophetic voice in the city' collects the meditations of Cardinal Carlo Maria Martini, archbishop of Milan, presented August 1993 in Caracas during the course of spiritual exercises for the clergy of Venezuela"—Foreword.
    ISBN 0-8146-2412-X
    1. Bible.   O. T.   Jeremiah–Meditations.   I. Title.
BS1525.4.M3713   1997
242'.692—dc21   97-14655
                                                            CIP

Contents

Foreword

A Prophetic Voice in the City collects the meditations of Cardinal Carlo Maria Martini, archbishop of Milan, presented August 1993 in Caracas during the course of spiritual exercises for the clergy of Venezuela.

The prophetic voice is that of Jeremiah, one of the most important figures in the history of religion. The term "voice" indicates something human, audible, while the adjective "prophetic" alludes to the fact that it pronounces words of God, whether threatening or consoling, but in any case directed toward converting the hearts of men and women, to convert the city.

Jeremiah, a sorrowful and loving friend of God, steeped in a strong passionate love of the One who called him to be his voice in the midst of the people, is a great solitary. Misunderstood and persecuted, scorned even by the members of his family, he does not marry or become a father; imprisoned and tortured for his oracles, then sent to Egypt, he will die in a distant land where no news will be left as to his tomb's whereabouts. Yet he was not by nature a hard or solitary man. Being so was imposed upon him by a violent external force that nagged and gripped him; one that demanded total obedience because it needed his solitude as a means of action within the people of Judea. This force was the word. There is no other prophet who evokes the word of God and the divine way of acting with the same painful precision of Jeremiah: "Your words were found, and I ate them, and your words became to me a joy . . ." (Jer 15:16). And later: "For the word of the LORD has become for me a reproach and derision all day long" (Jer 20:8b). He himself will be a fire consuming the recalcitrant people.

Living in the tragic period in which the destruction of the reign of Judea was prepared and accomplished, he is sent "to pluck up, break down, and destroy" (Jer 18:7); although wishing for peace—in his natural meekness and sensitivity—he must fight against his very own, against the kings, the priests, the false prophets. His solitude is strictly tied, therefore, to the content of the message entrusted to him: the existence or non-existence of all things depends on God. Torn apart by the mission entrusted to him, yet incapable of eschewing it, Jeremiah is purified by this very form of suffering. In the interior contact with God, his understanding of the importance of the heart in the relationship of faith and in the obedience to the covenant brings him to abandon himself completely to the Lord, to hope against every hope in a future of reconciliation of humanity with God.

The oracles pronounced against the false securities in the political and religious arenas, and the oracles against all the nations must open hearts to a new covenant, much more vast than the first.

The present volume is not an exegetical commentary on the Book of Jeremiah, neither is it a continuous reading of the fifty-two chapters as they are proposed by the Bible; it does not even dwell on the numerous provocations springing from the text.

Cardinal Martini has simply preferred to delve deeply into some astounding excerpts from the prophet that are especially appropriate for pursuing the dynamics essential to spiritual exercises: namely, to purify the heart, to free it from all slavery, and to find the will of God. In other words, to put order in one's own life, the order willed by God, which humankind does not understand nor is able to follow precisely because it is not free. One must find the will of God in the context of a city divided, idolatrous, bewildered, humiliated, and wounded as Jerusalem was in the time of Jeremiah and as our cities are today. How can one still be a prophetic voice, and just what does it mean?

We are invited to reflect on our resistance to the beneficial and merciful action of God; on the motives for which we abandon God and his project of salvation; on our sins as a betrayal of the covenant; on the passion of Jeremiah and on his undisputed and unswerving faithfulness to the word; on the passages of consolations of the prophet, for which the whole book was actually written; passages that open the horizons to a vast and universal hope, which is the new covenant.

At the end of these meditations, just as at the end of the book of the prophet, we will come to understand that the only serious and true attitude for humanity is to place all spiritual values in the forefront, to abandon oneself with loving trust to divine action, even and especially in the suffering of a people and of a city, to live the strength and the joy of the word of the Lord.

Introduction

I have come here among you, thanks to the invitation of Cardinal José Ali Lebrún, archbishop of Caracas, who, on the occasion of his fiftieth anniversary to the priesthood, wished to experience a few days of spiritual exercises together with the priests and auxiliary bishops of the diocese.

I have gladly accepted the invitation in order to express my friendship and affection to him; also because I consider it a true gift of the Lord to be able to spend a time of silence with all of you, listening to the word, a time of prayer and contemplation.

I would, therefore, like to start with a prayer suggested to me by the short reading proclaimed in the third hour of the Divine Office, taken from the central passage of the book of the prophet Jeremiah: "But this is the covenant that I will make with the house of Israel after those days, says the LORD: I will put my law within them and I will write it on their hearts" (Jer 31:33).

> We praise and thank you, Lord, because you have made a covenant with us, with our people; you have made a covenant with the Church of Venezuela, with the Church of Milan; you have made a covenant with the whole Catholic Church scattered throughout the world, in communion with our highest pontiff, John Paul II.
>
> We thank you, Lord, for the gift of the covenant and even though the problems are many, we feel secure and trusting as we rest in it. You know the many and painful problems of my city of Milan, and those of Caracas. For this we pray that in these days of spiritual exercises, you might renew your law in

our hearts, inscribe it in our lives. Grant, Father, that through silence, listening to the word and in meditation, we may come to discover that you write in us that law of yours that is a reality of love, and that you rewrite it at every moment through the grace of the Holy Spirit. We ask you to inscribe it also for all our people, our parishes and dioceses, so that we can all proclaim that you are our God and we are your people. Listen to our prayer, Father, through Jesus Christ your Son our Lord and through the intercession of the Virgin Mary. Amen.

The Purpose of the Exercises

What do we expect from the exercises? In the letter sent by Cardinal Lebrún to the diocese, our expectations are very well described: "That we, priests and bishops, can be truly men of God, that we trust in Him and rely on the strength of our supernatural mission." And so this is our intent: to be truly men of God.

And furthermore: that we "in an attitude of love and service, can announce to all that God loves them and that it is his will that humankind live in brotherhood . . . as we attempt to live during these days of exercises in dialogue with God, in attentive listening, in the silence of prayer and supplication, in order to revive our love and our dedication to Jesus, and our loyalty to the Church that is a sign and bond of union of God's love for humankind."

These words of the Cardinal summarize well the plan we wish to accomplish with the help of God.

The Prophet Jeremiah

1. I will propose certain meditations, following the method of *lectio divina,* on the prophet Jeremiah.

I have chosen Jeremiah because he is a difficult prophet to understand; I have already meditated on him during a course of spiritual exercises with the seminarians of the diocese of

Milan, but I chose to return to him so as to capture his thought more deeply. I will confess, in fact, that I have been struggling with Jeremiah for many years without fully understanding him; I will probably still need much more time. I will simply try to utter something on his book that comprises fifty-two chapters, the longest book in the Bible after Isaiah.

But there is another reason for my choice: wishing to honor the fiftieth anniversary to the priesthood of Cardinal Lebrún, it seemed appropriate to meditate on a prophetic existence, also taking into consideration that the prophet Jeremiah lived in very obscure times. I feel in a certain way like his fellow traveler because in Milan we are living in very harsh times. Aside from the events of "bribery city," involving all the political figures of the past forty years, we have witnessed some vicious attacks that have brought harm to victims in the way. I think that Jeremiah can help me and us to move through dramatic and distressing situations.

As Father Alonso Schökel well describes in the preface to his translation of Jeremiah: "No prophet has put so much of his life in his writings." Therefore, he comforts and consoles us with his personal tragic existence.

Finally, and most of all, we will reflect on the prophet because Jeremiah is one of the paths to knowing Jesus better.

When Jesus asked his apostles "Who do people say that the Son of Man is?," they answered: "Some say John the Baptist, but others Elijah, and still others Jeremiah or one of the prophets" (Matt 16:13-14).

Among the figures instinctively associated with Jesus by the people is Jeremiah, not the great Isaiah or Ezekiel or Daniel.

2. Obviously, we cannot perform a continuous reading of the whole book, and we will have to be content with some pages from it. I wondered how to best resolve the problem of the order of the readings. One could, for instance, read Jeremiah according to a biographical scheme, following the events of his life, even if the book seems like a disorderly pile

of disparate elements. The biographical plan would have us consider the various ages of the prophet: from 0 to 18 (the time of his vocation), from 18 to 36 (the prophecies under Josiah), from 36 to 48 (the prophecies under Joachim) and so on until his death. But I do not believe such an order to be useful because the facts are all very general and in any case difficult to link with the content of the text.

Another hypothesis is to follow the chronological order of the oracles, some of which are dated. For example, in chapter 1:2: ". . . to whom the word of the LORD came in the days of King Josiah son of Amon in the thirteenth year of his reign." We are, therefore, in 628 or 627 B.C., and Jeremiah was 18–19 years old. Also in chapter 3:6 we find a date, albeit a very generic one: "The LORD said to me in the days of King Josiah . . ." and Josiah reigned from 628 to 609 B.C. Chapter 14 speaks of a great society and certain circumstances that remind one of the end of King Josiah's reign, toward 609. On the other hand, compared to the hundreds of oracles the book comprises, the dated ones are too few to elaborate a satisfactory chronological order.

I have also thought of using the logical line, the order of the texts of the book. To clarify with a comparison, let us remember, in this regard, the Gospel of Matthew, composed of sections of sermons and sections of stories: the Sermon on the Mount (chs. 5–7); stories of miracles (chs. 8–9); the missionary sermon (ch. 10); various stories (chs. 11–12), etc. The Book of Jeremiah was composed according to a sequence of this kind: a first section of sermons (chs. 1–25 of oracles); a narrative section (chs. 26–29); another series of sermons, among which I emphasize the one on the new covenant (chs. 30–33); again a narrative section due mostly to Baruch, the secretary (chs. 34–35); a section of sermons (chs. 46–52). We have, therefore, three sections of oracles, separated by two narrative sections.

This, however, is the only sure thing that can be said about the logical order of the prophet's words; if we try instead to look for a logical order within the section, it is almost impossible to find it.

In conclusion, it seems to me that the book must be compared to a group of mosaic chips that have never been put together, so that we find chips of one color where those of another color should be, and vice versa. Every piece, every chip, has its own beauty, yet it is difficult to visualize a total design. Or we can compare the pages that go under the name of the prophet Jeremiah to a quarry of piled-up diamonds; one must first get them out, then place them in some order. It seems to me almost impossible to do a *lectio continua* of Jeremiah that would have a precise, logical order.

The Dynamism of the Meditations

We will then read the book as one would use a stockpile of pearls or precious stones, taking as we go along those that attract and interest us, the ones that speak to us. The order we will follow is simply the dynamic order of the exercises that I express in a synthetic way: to purify oneself in order to find the will of God.

There are some very beautiful oracles of Jeremiah on the purification of the heart (the first part of the exercises); we will choose some of the more poetic images to help us penetrate into the mystery of the purification of the heart (let us remember that Jeremiah is a superb poet!). Then I will read other oracles that show us the will of God. After all, the spiritual exercises simply tend to purify our hearts so that we can find the divine will and comply to it, attempting to answer the question: What does God ask of me today and how should I purify my heart and mind to know his will and carry it out with love?

The first two meditations that I am suggesting will have an introductory character to the path of the exercises, always having Jeremiah's texts as a point of departure; then we will enter into the meditations of purification and subsequently into those seeking the divine will.

I like to think of the path we will pursue as a lovely walk in a forest full of unknown trees, of birds of every kind and color; it is the forest of Jeremiah's images, and we will pick now a flower, then a fruit; at times we will stop to look at a tree or a bird, gradually becoming familiar with the life and person of this extraordinary prophet.

Three Required Attitudes for the Exercises

You already know what is required of whoever wishes to pursue the spiritual exercises: to communal moments of *lectio divina,* personal prayer must follow, the dialogue with God in an attitude of adoration, prayer and the pursuit and in-depth study of biblical passages.

I would, however, like to underline three attitudes that find a parallel in the Scriptures and against which I invite you to measure yourselves so as to better experience these days.

1. The attitude of diligent servant, who fulfills his duty well. It is the attitude of the person who has made a commitment with the Lord and with himself to perform the exercises well and to totally experience prayer, silence, listening and reading. The level of the diligent servant is important. It is satisfying because one can say, I have listened well, I have been patient, I have gathered some merit. He who does the exercises as a diligent servant puts his life in order, makes a good confession, and lives a moment of spiritual balance. But, we are not yet in a perfect attitude; in fact, the faithful servant draws no happiness from his diligence.

2. The second is the attitude of the faithful friend, namely of the individual who is not only concerned with being diligent, but also wants to enter into the Lord's intentions: "Lord, what do you want of me during these exercises, what do you ask of me? What is your plan for me?" While the first attitude puts us in balance, the one of faithful friend disposes us to change our lives. However, we usually do not truly change them, but it makes us understand what we should change, it makes us desire it.

3. The attitude of the ecstatic lover truly changes one's life. We cannot obtain this merely on our own, but God has prepared it for us as a special grace. I see the passage leading from diligent servant to ecstatic lover in the parable of the talents, where it is said that when the Lord returns, he who had received five talents brings five more saying: "Master, you handed over to me five talents; see, I have made five more talents." The Lord answers: "Well done, good and trustworthy slave; you have been trustworthy in a few things, I will put you in charge of many things; enter into the joy of your master" (Matt 25:20-21).

It is the attitude of the person who lives the exercises not only as a diligent servant, as a faithful friend who tries to understand what the Lord wants, but as one who enters into the feast of his Lord. This person enters into the exercises to give glory to God, so that God may rejoice in what he does and in his prayer and takes pleasure in what he desires and in the gifts he gives him.

Again, I say, this seems to be the only attitude that really changes us, because it makes us forget ourselves, our tiredness, our toils, our worries, to enter into the joy of the Lord. It is, as I said, a grace, but God prepares it for all Christians and especially for his priests. To be able to exult in reciting a psalm, reading a biblical text or placing oneself in adoration of the Blessed Sacrament: I delight, O Lord, in giving joy to you, in being part of your glory; it means living the resurrection of Christ, and we are, in fact, in the time of joy and resurrection.

However, I am also here among you to learn, and for this purpose we will have in the evenings moments of communication in our faith. I will also be happy to meet you personally because I know that your experiences will enrich me. One of the very reasons, in fact, that attracts me to preaching the exercises to other Churches is the possibility of benefiting from the lessons that the Holy Spirit gives me.

The Action of God

I have explained what my part and yours will be during these exercises. And what will God do? The prophet Jeremiah explains it to us: "The word of the LORD came to me, saying, 'Jeremiah, what do you see?' And I said: 'I see a branch of an almond tree.' The LORD said to me: 'You have seen well, for I am watching over my word to perform it'" (Jer 1:11).

> We thank you, Lord, because you watch over your word; it is not so much we who look for the word in order to understand it, but you who give it to us so it can enter into our hearts. Grant us, we pray, an open and docile heart as we allow you to watch over us. You care lovingly for each one of us, for the Church and for all humanity, and you do not let any of your words fall in vain. Let us welcome them with that same love you infuse in the words you give us, through the intercession of Mary our Mother and in the name of Jesus your Son and our Lord. Amen.

1.

In the Potter's Shop

In the *Spiritual Exercises* of St. Ignatius of Loyola, before starting the actual meditations, one reflects on No. 23, entitled *Principle and Foundation,* as a point of departure from the path.

I have asked myself which is the page of Jeremiah that can correspond to this *Principle and Foundation,* that could serve as a cornerstone on which the building can be built. To this purpose, I've found that the section which I would call "In the Potter's Shop" to be very significant.

The Principle and Foundation of Jeremiah

The word that came to Jeremiah from the LORD: "Come, go down to the potter's house, and there I will let you hear my words." So I went down to the potter's house and there he was working at his wheel. The vessel he was making of clay was spoiled in the potter's hand, and he reworked it into another vessel, as seemed good to him.

Then the word of the LORD came to me: Can I not do with you, O house of Israel, just as this potter has done? says the LORD. Just like the clay in the potter's hand, so are you in my hand, O house of Israel. At one moment I may declare concerning a nation or a kingdom, that I will pluck up and break down and destroy it, but if that nation, concerning which I have spoken, turns from its evil, I will change my mind about the disaster that I intended to bring on it. And at another moment I may declare concerning a nation or a kingdom that I will build and plant it, but if it does evil in my sight, not listening to my voice, then I will change my mind about the good that I had intended to do to it. Now, therefore, say to the people of Judah and the inhabitants of Jerusalem: Thus says the LORD: Look, I am a potter shaping evil against you and devising a plan against you. Turn now, all of you from your evil way, and amend your ways and your doings.

But they say, "It is no use! We will follow our own plans, and each of us will act according to the stubbornness of our evil will" (Jer 18:1-12).

We will consider this page in its unity and we will meditate on it according to its triple traditional division of the Church: *lectio, meditatio,* and *contemplatio.* In the *lectio* we will slowly reread the passage so as to emphasize its more meaningful elements; often we think we already know a biblical text, but if we subject it to a systematic rereading, we then notice it contains a treasure never before discovered. In the *meditatio* we will ask ourselves what the message of the text is and finally, in the *contemplatio,* we will enter into dialogue with God who speaks to us, to each and everyone of us.

Lectio of Jeremiah 18:1-12

1. In what historical period did this oracle occur? Since in verse 11 the Lord says, "I am a potter shaping evil against you and devising a plan against you," it can then be considered pronounced before the great punishment, the invasion of Jerusalem that occurred in 590 B.C. Very generally it can be said to belong to the first or second period of the prophet's life, when he was between 35 and 45 years old.

The passage in fact refers to certain characteristics pertaining to Jeremiah's vocation that are already known and accepted. Let us observe, for instance, the verbs in verse 7: "I will pluck up and break down and destroy it," and those of verse 9: "I may declare that I will build and plant it." They are the same verbs that define the prophet's vocation in chapter 1:10:

> See, today I appoint you over
>   nations and over kingdoms,
> to pluck and to pull down,
> to destroy and to overthrow,
> to build and to plant.

So these are already traditional verbs to indicate the ministry of Jeremiah.

We cannot, however, be more specific about the time-frame.

2. It is then important to try to read the passage according to the division of its parts, to see how it is structured and to understand it in its internal dynamics.

Basically, there are two parts:

a) the first (vv. 1-4) contains the mysterious order imposed on the prophet and the carrying out of the order. It is a totally symbolic, enigmatic part and without comments; God orders, Jeremiah executes, but one does not understand what is spoken of.

b) The second (vv. 5-12) is the oracle explaining the action and it is in turn divided into three phases.

—The oracle itself is expressed in question form: "Can I not do with you, O House of Israel, just as the potter has done?" and then in an affirmative form: "Just like the clay in the potter's hand, so are you in my hand" (v. 6). This is the focal point of the whole oracle.

—In a second phase, the oracle is explained in a negative form (v. 7: pluck up, break down, and destroy) and in a positive form (v. 9: build and plant). As if to say: the Lord accomplishes what he wishes, he destroys and builds.

—After the explanation, there is the moment of application (vv. 11-12) to the people of Judea and the inhabitants of Jerusalem: "Look, I am shaping evil against you and devising a plan against you. Turn now all of you from your evil way. . . ." We will call this the hortatory part.

The text is, therefore, solidly composed, and Jeremiah probably described the incident as he experienced it. After 2,500 years, we still feel the dramatic force of the prophetic experience; he must prophesy on his city, at the cost of his life; he is the prophet of his own destiny, not of events that don't pertain to him.

It is interesting that the text is all based on images of the potter. When I was in Jerusalem once, I went to an old neighborhood and had the opportunity to visit a potter's shop. The man turned the lathe via a pedal, and taking in his hand some muddy, soft clay, he placed it on the turntable and shaped it. The clay turned and, through the fingers' touch, it was shaped into a vase. When the vase does not turn out well, then the clay is thrown back into the batch and reworked.

Jeremiah observes the artist, contemplates him as we would do today if we saw a potter working at his craft; he then understands he must let himself be shaped, molded by the divine potter.

3. I cannot comment on the page word for word, but I will simply underline the focal point: "Just like the clay in the potter's hand, so are you in my hand" (Jer 18:6b). This, in my view, is the central word of God, the prophetic intuition: we are in the hands of God like clay in the potter's hand. We will take this theme up again in the moment of the *meditatio*. But in the meantime, I wish to recall that such an intuition is very frequent in the Bible.

—For example, it happens in two important passages of the Book of Isaiah:

> Shall the potter be regarded as the clay?
> Shall the thing made say of its maker,
>   "He did not make me?"
> or the thing formed say of the one who formed it,
>   "He has no understanding?" (Isa 29:16).

It is a concept intimately tied to the theme of creation. When humankind loses its sense of creatureliness, it becomes mad, wants to overturn the roles, and presumes to tell God how to act (like the vase saying to the potter: "You don't understand!") It is the overturning of the creatureliness typical of contemporary, atheistic society: to forget that humans are made by God, and to deny the very foundation of Christian anthropology.

—And again:

> Woe to you who strive with your Maker,
>> earthen vessels with the potter!
> Does the clay say to the one who fashions it, "What are you
>> making?"
>> or: "Your work has no handles?" (Isa 45:9)

The product, the creature, believes it is possible to dictate the laws of its own existence.

—The metaphor of the potter is found in other scriptural texts, but has its origins in the story of Genesis 2:7: ". . . then the LORD God formed man from the dust of the ground. . . ." Man is formed by God, who "breathed into his nostrils the breath of life" and let him become a living being. This is the principle of the true vision of the world.

—Paul himself will recapture the image in his Letter to the Romans, for example:

> But who indeed are you, a human being, to argue with God? Will what is molded say to one who molds it, "Why have you made me like this?" Has the potter no right over the clay, to make out of the same lump one object for special use and another for ordinary use? (Rom 9:20-21).

—The theme of creatureliness, so entrenched in the biblical Hebraic tradition, is an essential point of reference when speaking of humankind and of God.

Meditatio: The Message of Jeremiah

Now that we have reread the page of Jeremiah, let us turn to the meditatio, wishing to capture the message for us, for our culture, our Church, and our civilization.

Of course each individual must ask What is the message for me in these exercises? And the best answer can be found in prayer, in reading and rereading the text, also in the light of Isaiah, Genesis, and the letter to the Romans. But the beauty of the *lectio divina* lies in the fact that by meditating on a passage, our memory is instinctively able to recall other ones. The *lectio divina* lets us walk through the meadows of Scripture, allowing us to string pearl after pearl, so that these jewel-like words mutually reinforce each other and help us to have the sense of God's world and to enter into the mystery of his word.

I am now suggesting three paths of reflections for the meditation.

1. The first is taken from Psalm 100:3, which expresses the image of the potter in a direct form. It is a psalm of praise and of entrance into prayer:

> Know that the LORD is God.
>> It is he that made us, and we are his;
>> we are his people, and the sheep of his pasture.

Interesting also is Psalm 96:5, 8, 9:

> For all the gods of the peoples are idols,
>> but the LORD made the heavens. . . .

> Ascribe to the LORD the glory due his name . . .

> Worship the LORD in holy splendor . . .

> Say among the nations, "The LORD is king!"

These are all ways to affirm the decisive gesture of human life that consists in recognizing that we belong to God, all ways of expressing the fundamental religious gesture of adoration. The difference between those who believe and those who do not lies mostly in the capacity—or lack of it—to adore. During the past few weeks, I was particularly struck by the suicide of two famous men in Italy who had everything in life: money, career, and success. Accused by the judges or fearing accusation, they were not able to endure, hence they killed themselves. Yet, there are other persons who live with hope, even if they risk prison or trial. How is this possible? Of course it is not up to us to judge, because suicide is probably the result of despair, exasperation, and the loss of the ability to exercise free will; nevertheless, at least one of the two persons mentioned was an agnostic with no belief in eternal life. If one loses the thought of being in the hands of God, when despair comes, no other viable option remains except death. For this reason I believe adoration is fundamental: to know how to adore, to know that I am in the hands of one who is greater than myself.

People in Venezuela are still basically very religious precisely because they know how to adore; in Europe, on the other hand, people are indifferent. They no longer have the sense of creatureliness that is at the root of prayer and of liturgy, the sense of morality lived as morality based on Revelation.

> I thank you, my Lord and my God, because I can adore you; it is a great gift to adore you; it is a great gift that changes the optics of existence. I adore you, my God, and with joy I want to repeat this act that places me in my true status as creature.

2. A second path of reflection, suggested by Jeremiah, is that I can resist God's action, I can escape from the hands of the potter who is forming me.

The vase that we are has the dramatic power to resist God who is forming it. Each of us is, therefore, co-responsible for his or her destiny and life, for good or for bad.

However, the great principle of creation marking a responsible dependency, the element of freedom introduced in Jeremiah's metaphor, means also that God is co-responsible with me for what he has placed in my hands; hence, not everything weighs solely on me.

This is the comforting aspect of co-responsibility. The individual who does not believe, but is a serious, honest, and loyal person who feels deeply life's responsibility, feels that everything has to weigh on his or her shoulders; at a certain point, this could mean being crushed by it; so if this person commits any mistake, there will be self-blaming. But one who has faith knows that even when making mistakes, there is a potter ready to help, and hence there is no need to be alone. Because God, who does nothing without our freedom, does everything for us if we want it; he will always sustain us and share our path that is difficult and laden with errors.

I am personally relieved and consoled by this certainty; my pastoral responsibilities do not frighten me because of my trust in the Lord who shares them, that it is God who forms my mission, my life, and my future. It is God who forms a diocese, who shapes the Church, and we must let ourselves be shaped. His mercy knows how to recover the clay thrown back into the muddy heap and to form it into the masterpiece he wishes, to restore us to his love.

As I was writing an article on suicide in our weekly diocesan paper, I was saying that if these people would have known and understood Jeremiah's teachings, they would not have gone to such extremes. God is not frightened by the life of an individual who is corrupt, accused, tried, and jailed. For God, no human being is ever totally lost.

This text of Jeremiah has, therefore, a great value for today's society, for all those who feel the weight of their responsibilities (ecological, planetary, world hunger, for the future of humanity). God is with us, close to us, ready to offer us new opportunities; even a punishment is an act of mercy; even a failure in life, a sin, or a mistake can be changed by God into good.

The image of Jeremiah is truly splendid, a theological synthesis of the relationship between God and humanity, between creation and freedom, and between responsibility, sin, and redemption.

Contemplatio

The third division of the *lectio divina*, the *contemplatio*, is the part with which each of us needs to be involved; it consists in no longer reflecting on the text, but in placing oneself in an attitude of prayer.

Lord, I adore you because you have formed me thus. I often complain of the way you have shaped me, and I would almost want to ask you why: Why did you not give me the gifts I wanted? Why did you not give me certain possibilities? I ask your forgiveness, my God, and I am sure that you want to make of me your masterpiece if I place myself with complete trust in your hands.

And in prayer, we can review our lives with its errors, its failures, its mistakes:

Lord, I am in all ways yours. I belong to you, and I know that whatever seems wrong to me is simply placed there by you as an act of mercy for the future.

Let's allow our prayer to flow freely from our hearts, and let us contemplate the metaphor of the potter, applying it also to the Church, to the people of God. Just as God forms this Church, so also can God reject it, because in the prophet's image there is also the negative part, the threat.

Let us think of many Churches of the New Testament no longer in existence today, that have been thrown back into the muddy heap of clay: the Church of Ephesus, for example, of Laodicea, of Antioch of Cilicia, and of Antioch of Syria. They were clay masterpieces and have since disappeared. So what is left of the sites where Paul preached? Eternity is assured to the Church, not to the Churches. Individual Churches share the responsibility for their future; their survival is tied to their response. The Lord has allowed the Church of Augustine, of Cyprian and, of Ignatius of Antioch to fall away and disappear.

Therefore, history is serious and is entrusted to us. But God destroys here and builds there because he is the Lord of the Church and of history:

Lord, you are the Lord of the Venezuelan Church, of the Church of Caracas, of the Church of Milan; you are the Lord of the Latin American and European Churches. You want to re-build those Churches in difficulty, if we first of all live in a deep sense of adoration, if we feel to be humbly in your hands.

Here is a last suggestion for your personal prayer. You will perhaps feel some resistance in adoring God's plans for your life, your Church, and your country; such resistance is already recorded in Scripture: "Why," says the vase to the potter, "did you make me in this manner?"

Allow such resistance to take on its own voice in order to fully reveal itself, purify it in prayer, and be able then to enter into the great mystery of creation, which is our point of departure for our path of spiritual exercises.

HOMILY

Monday of the Eighteenth Week in Ordinary Time, Cycle I

Collaborators with God

We now want to read over certain passages that have been chosen in the context of the meditation regarding our individual, personal responsibility and our co-responsibility with God for the task entrusted to us.

The Responsibility of Moses

> The rabble among them had a strong craving; and the Israelites also wept again, and said, "If only we had meat to eat! We remember the fish we used to eat in Egypt for nothing, the cucumbers, the melons, the leeks, the onions, and the garlic; but now our strength is dried up, and there is nothing at all but this manna to look at. . . ."
>
> Moses heard the people weeping throughout their families, all at the entrances of their tents. Then the LORD became very angry, and Moses was displeased. So Moses said to the LORD, "Why have you treated your servant so badly? Why have I not found favor in your sight, that you lay the burden of all this people on me? Did I conceive all this people? . . . Where am I to get meat to give to all this people? For they come weeping to me and say, 'Give us meat to eat!' I am not able to carry all this people alone, for they are too heavy for me. If this is the way you are going to treat me, put me to death at once" (Num 11:4-15).

In this excerpt, emphasis is placed on the responsibility of Moses, who cannot answer everything that is asked of him; the people entrusted to him are difficult, demanding and prone to complaining.

How does Moses come out of this situation of overwhelming responsibility? Through discovering the basic function of his being: intercession. We are facing here one of the many Pentateuch texts in which he appears as a man of prayer, who speaks to the Lord in the name of the people and intercedes so intensely that he almost comes to arguing with his God: "Why have you treated your servant so badly? Why have I not found favor in your sight . . . ?"

Moses, who is guiding Israel through the desert after passing through the Red Sea, feels all the weight of his responsibility and wishes to share it with the Lord. Thanks to this heartfelt invocation that results from much suffering and also excessive toil, he slowly regains the truth of his life, the serenity, the trust, and the right conscience of his ministry of mediator and pastor; his role is to share the responsibility of the people with God.

And we are invited to reflect on our responsibilities that are well clarified in the figure of Moses.

Jesus and the Disciples

In the gospel passage of the multiplication of the loaves (Matt 14:13-21), Jesus in the same way arouses his disciples to face their responsibility. Night is falling, the crowds surrounding Jesus are large, the disciples advise him to dismiss them so that everyone can eat, and Jesus replies: "You give them something to eat." With these words, he wants to try them; if they accept this burden upon their shoulders, they will be crushed by it, but if they share it with him, allowing him to guide the situation, they will be able to recapture the function of givers of Bread and of the word: "He broke the loaves and gave them to the disciples, and the disciples gave them to the crowds."

The disciples, the apostles, have recaptured their just place of mediators, not attempting to avoid their responsibilities, because they understand that they carry them with the Lord. The right place is indicated by the verb "intercede," which means "to be in the middle of," to walk between God and the people, knowing that one is a mere collaborator in the divine plan of salvation.

And we, too, find ourselves in the middle in the moment of the Eucharist that marks the apex of each day of ours. We are not alone, in fact, but with our people, our parishes, our dioceses; we can never be cut off from the people, nor forget them. So this presence allows us to feel even more the Lord's presence as he says to each of us: "I carry this weight of the ministry with you, and if you have only five loaves and two fish to respond to the people's needs, do not worry; bring them to me with them and I will give you nourishment for all."

> Lord, grant us to live our intercession, to always know how to be at the right place, neither outside of our responsibilities nor crushed by them, in the certainty that you, God, creator and Lord, take care of your people and of us.
>
> We, therefore, entrust to you these five loaves and two fish that are our exercises, our challenge for these days we are experiencing, our humble patience, so that you may change them into bread for all the men and women who are hungry; we ask that you change them into nourishment of the body and of the spirit for millions of people living in our cities; for all those in the world who hunger and thirst for God.

2.

The Broken Jug

The Path of Purification of the Heart

In chapter 19 of Jeremiah, we contemplate the symbol of the broken jug that is connected, also because of the object, to the other great symbol of the vase and the potter. The image is, therefore, similar to the preceding one, but with an important difference. While, in fact, the earthenware vase can be re-shaped if its shape is not well-turned, the symbol that we are considering today is that of a human situation that once degenerated is rejected, and is then destroyed. The reflection on the broken jug goes even deeper; it goes further into human evil, it presents us with something destructive to humanity, namely sin.

The previous meditation recalled the principle and foundation of Jeremiah's life and ours. Now we must devote ourselves, according to the pattern of the spiritual exercises, to the purification of the heart, contemplating the pages of Jeremiah dealing with sin and its consequences, the breaking of the covenant and whatever cannot be accepted into human history because it ruins it.

We will see in chapter 19 that Jeremiah performs a prophetic act. We will start by rereading the text as we attempt to capture its rather intricate, internal structure, in order to then understand the message it brings to our modern cities, abandoned to a secular and idolatrous dynamism. We will ask ourselves how these destructive forces operate there as well as in the secularist city of our heart.

The Broken Jug

Thus said the LORD: Go and buy a potter's earthenware jug. Take with you some of the elders of the people and some of the senior priests, and go out to the valley of the son of Hinnom at the entry of the Potsherd Gate, and proclaim there the words that I tell you. You shall say: Hear the word of the LORD, O kings of Judah and inhabitants of Jerusalem. Thus says the LORD of hosts, the God of Israel: I am going to bring such disaster upon this place that the ears of everyone who hears of it will tingle. Because the people have forsaken me, and have profaned this place by making offerings in it to other gods whom neither they nor their ancestors nor the kings of Judah have known; and because they have filled this place with the blood of the innocent, and gone on building the high places of Baal to burn their children in the fire as burnt offerings to Baal, which I did not command or decree, nor did it enter my mind. Therefore the days are surely coming, says the LORD, when this place shall no more be called Topheth, or the valley of the son of Hinnom, but the valley of Slaughter. And in this place I will make void the plans of Judah and Jerusalem, and will make them fall by the sword of their enemies, and by the hand of those that seek their life. I will give their dead bodies for food to the birds of the air and to the wild animals of the earth. And I will make this city a horror, a thing to be hissed at; everyone who passes by it will be horrified and will hiss because of all its disasters. And I will make them eat the flesh of their sons and the flesh of their daughters, and all shall eat the flesh of their neighbors in the siege, and in the distress with which their enemies and those who seek their life afflict them.

Then you shall break the jug in the sight of those who go with you, and shall say to them: Thus says the LORD of hosts: So will I break this people and this city, as one breaks a potter's vessel, so that it can never be mended. In Topheth they shall bury until there is no more room to bury. Thus will I do to this place, says the LORD, and to its inhabitants, making this city like Topheth.

And the houses of Jerusalem and the houses of the kings of Judah shall be defiled like the place of Topheth—all the houses upon whose roofs offerings have been made to the whole host of heaven, and libations have been poured out to other gods.

When Jeremiah came from Topheth, where the LORD had sent him to prophesy, he stood in the court of the LORD's house and said to all the people: Thus says the LORD of hosts, the God of Israel: I am now bringing upon this city and upon all its towns all the disaster that I have pronounced against it, because they have stiffened their necks, refusing to hear my words (Jer 19:1-15).

The words of this prophetic action are very harsh and strong, and remind us of certain expressions pronounced by Jesus on Jerusalem in his eschatological talk (cf. Matt 24:15-25), as well as the weeping over Jerusalem ("As [Jesus] came near and saw the city, he wept over it . . ." Luke 19:41). Jeremiah's words, resonating in the very life of Jesus, illustrated, the situation of a city that abandons God and searches for itself.

Lectio of Jeremiah 19:1-15

1. This difficult and composite passage seems also a bit disorganized, so much so that interpreters have tried to rewrite it. I see, for instance, that the edition of the *Nueva Biblia Española*, used by you, reads it in a different order, placing the verses of the chapter in another order. The interpreters, in fact, consider the hypothesis that chapter 19 may mix together two stories, two oracles.

Oracle a) would be the symbolic action of the prophet at the door called Potsherd Gate; Jeremiah, through God's order, takes a jug and breaks it. Then he goes to the temple and explains his action, pronouncing the oracle against the city (vv. 1-2, 10).

Oracle b) would instead include a speech to the city proclaimed in the valley of the Son of Hinnom (vv. 3-9, 11-13). The likely confusion is caused by verse 2: ". . . go out to the valley of the son of Hinnom at the entry of the Potsherd Gate." Perhaps two sites are in question: one is the valley of the son of Hinnom, where the oracle against the city is pronounced; the other is the entry of the Potsherd Gate, where the jug is broken and then the commentary is made about the breakage as an oracle against Jerusalem.

I will not belabor this reconstruction, since we must read the text as it is transmitted to us. There are, however, two oracles on the same theme, and it is understandable that the final compiler of the Book of Jeremiah placed them together.

2. The text presents a double parallel rhythm: there is a command to do and a command to say; then there is a second command to do and a second command to say:

—vv. 1-2a: The Lord tells Jeremiah to buy the earthenware jug and to go to a certain place in the city. It is a command to do an action and, as in the story of the potter, it remains mysterious and enigmatic.

—v. 3: "You shall say: Hear the word of the LORD." It is a command to tell a rather long oracle, and we will go deeper into the main point, found in verse 4.

—v. 10: "You shall break the jug. . . ." After the action to buy, there is another action, namely, the one to break the purchased jug.

—v. 11: There follows an order to say something: "And [you] shall say to them: Thus says the LORD of hosts."

It can be imagined that the execution of the command occurs in verse 14, because Jeremiah returns to the door where the Lord had sent him and stops in the entrance of the temple. In verse 15 we read the prophecy that concludes the chapter: "Thus says the LORD of hosts, the God of Israel: I am now bringing upon this city and upon all its towns all the disaster that I have pronounced against it, because they have stiffened their necks, refusing to hear my words."

3. Just when was this oracle pronounced and when did the symbolic gesture of the broken jug occur?

Almost surely around 605 B.C., namely, shortly before another dramatic event described in chapter 36: the destruction of the scroll of Jeremiah's prophecy, through action of the king. It is most probably this prophecy of chapter 19 that the king does not want to hear because it is so terrible that he throws it in the fire after having cut up its parchment into small pieces with a penknife.

Five Messages

I will forego reflecting on the message contained by the oracle for the prophet's contemporaries; one would have to situate it in the historical reality of idolatry, of decadence, of the unsuccessful reform of Josiah, of the relapse of the people at the time of Joachim, etc. What interests us is understanding the permanent messages of the text, read in the light of the mystery of Christ who died and rose from the dead. I have gathered here five such messages.

> Lord, grant us to receive in prayer your message for us. The words you have pronounced against your beloved city are very harsh and we ask you to let us understand what they mean today; what they mean for me, your city, your masterpiece. Allow me to participate in your suffering for the sins of humanity, in the suffering of Jesus for his city, for our cities.

1. I begin with a general reflection. The broken pitcher, made useless, unusable, only worthy of being thrown near the Potsherd Gate, underlines that there are human actions which cannot be healed, that not only are useless, but that are thrown out, rejected, unmasked. The prophet, therefore, points his finger to all destructive human actions. It is an especially strong message; we must not accept, take in, or absorb everything; there are actions that must be refused with utmost determination.

2. In verse 4 we have heard the description of these unacceptable situations needing to be unmasked: "Because the

people have forsaken me, and have profaned this place by making offerings in it to other gods, whom neither they nor their ancestors nor the kings of Judah have known; and because they have filled this place with the blood of the innocent."

—The first situation is that of the abandonment of God ("they have forsaken me"). God is no longer considered as the One who is the Lord of all of life.

—After the incredulity, idolatry is unmasked ("they have profaned this place by making offerings in it to other gods").

—Finally, the inhumanity (innocent blood).

Here we see an identification with sin, which consists precisely in not recognizing God as lord of life and of history, in adoring idols, and in becoming inhuman toward one's brothers.

There are three attitudes constituting the destructive and negative actions on which I would like to briefly comment.

a) The incredulity not only theoretic—atheism—but also practical. It happens when I do not recognize the power of God in my daily life, even if perhaps I repeat with my lips "Lord, Lord." God must be recognized as Lord of my actions, of my daily morals.

b) Idolatry is not necessarily the adoration of idols; according to the doctrine later specified in the New Testament, it is the adoration of success, of pleasure, of power at any cost, of money. Large modern cities are moved by such "gods."

It is an attitude that mirrors the abandonment of God: to refuse God as Lord is at the same time recognizing political power, worldly power, and wealth as lords of one's life.

c) Connected to the previous two is inhumanity, not being moved by the sufferings of another, using another, oppressing or despising the poor.

3. I would like you to notice that of these three sins, the most striking, the one that is horribly repellent, is inhumanity.

Let us observe how people are indignant in front of violence, oppression, injustice. Even a secular culture sees the most obvious face of sin in inhumanity.

Nevertheless, the secular city often doesn't realize that the contempt for one's brother, the hatred of another, often has its root in idolatry, namely the idolatry of self, of one's personal project, the adoration of money and of success. Inhumanity is only the third reason for the degradation, and here the message of Jeremiah's prophecy turns up appropriately. If we do not understand that the race to autonomy, to unbridled pleasure, to drugs, to wealth, to career, to power is evil . . . if we do not grasp how from all of this a dreadful humanity unfolds, it will be impossible to put an end to oppression and to the sufferings of others.

We must, therefore, help the secular city to better understand its idolatrous roots. But it is not enough, because idolatry, in turn, derives from faithlessness, from having forgotten who God is.

Human beings today do not accept the covenant or the Lord as an influential partner who is co-responsible for their destiny, the only one to love, to adore, to serve.

If our cities were able to focus their attention on the diabolical trio of faithlessness; idolatry-success-power; and inhumanity, they could more easily eradicate injustice and social sins.

Jeremiah's prophecy is very important because it goes to the root of evil and presents an extremely lucid analysis of what causes the disorder and decadence of nations. It also recalls three attitudes that produce irreparable situations, destined to self-destruct.

4. We underlined how large, modern cities, in their negative dynamics, have lost a sense of God and constantly focus on unbridled ambitions, hence becoming symbols of inhumanity.

In our hearts we feel the effects of certain words of Luke's gospel that we can translate thus: "Woe to you, secular city who counts on your riches, woe to you, unhappy city who enjoys a surfeit of pleasure, making of it an idol; woe to you who mocks others with sarcasm as if you lacked nothing, while actually you are lacking the most important thing; woe to you who puts all your desires in social and political success" (cf. Luke 6:24-26).

Jeremiah sees Jerusalem as a megalopolis that, forgetting God and becoming idolatrous, oppresses the poor; hence, his prophecy is a cry, since he knows that the city in this way annihilates itself.

What is, therefore, the meaning of our prophetic mission? It is to save the city, to tell the city what is the root of its sin and the source of its salvation.

In the past two years, in Italy, we have witnessed a political battle that has caused an ever-growing and pervasive corruption, giving rise to many forms of inhumanity.

The discovery of all this also means to discover the roots of a civilization's decadence, because a culture can build skyscrapers and great technical feats even if it is crumbling internally.

Jeremiah tries to save the city with his prophetic outcry; Jesus will save it by giving his life, dying for the city. Each one of us has the mission to become an intercessor like Jesus, to give one's life for one's own city.

As I conclude this fourth reflection, I ask myself: what is the opposite of the perverse trio (faithlessness, idolatry, and inhumanity)? The answer is easy: the Beatitudes, which represent the presence of God the king (blessed are the poor because the Lord shall be their king); they represent the just evaluation of moral goods (blessed are those who hunger and thirst for justice, blessed are the peacemakers); the Beatitudes are the triumph of humanity (blessed are the merciful), the proclamation that is in sharp contrast with the prophetic threats of Jeremiah.

Therefore, our prophetic preaching must (like Jeremiah's) point out and denounce, on the one hand, the great evils of the city, and, on the other, proclaim the Beatitudes as the salvation of the city, starting with the poor.

5. The secular city is within us, and we must recognize it; it would not exist outside if we did not have it within. "From the heart of man," says Jesus, evil actions and thoughts are born. Hence, a city that is without faith, is indifferent, idolatrous, and inhumane, would not exist if it did not already exist in our hearts.

We must then fight, above all, against the city within us, and examine ourselves to understand how much interior space it occupies.

—How much forgetfulness is there within me of the lordship of God?

> Lord, are you truly Lord of my life and my actions? Do I act in a way that obeys your will? (It is an examination on practical indifference).

—How much idolatry is there in us: desire for success, career, our special tastes, projects coveted as personal, unique ideals that we do not submit to the community or to the communion of others and of the Church? Let us reflect on all the divisions currently present in the Church that are caused by these idolatrous practices!

—Is there inhumanity in me or lack of attention to my brothers?

If we examine ourselves carefully, we will find in us at least some of the inhumanity displayed by the priests on the road to Jericho; they did not stop to help the wounded man because they were too preoccupied with themselves.

Therefore, we cannot be apostles in the secular city if we have not already driven out the hidden secular city within us. We often say we want to walk with the Lord, letting him live within us. But in reality we accept him as a guest to hold at bay, so as not to allow him to become master of our house. Today the Lord calls us to understand the roots of our self-love that are insurmountable and constantly regenerated. Sometimes these roots are disguised by religious motivation and forms of devotion; the Lord calls us to uproot them, so as to be transformed by his divine power.

"Purify me, O Lord"

For contemplative prayer, I suggest you recite Psalm 51, where in some way the psalmist picks up Jeremiah's themes:

Have mercy on me, O God,
>according to your steadfast love,
according to your abundant mercy
>blot out my transgressions.
Wash me thoroughly from my iniquity,
>and cleanse me from my sin.
For I know my transgressions,
>and my sin is ever before me.
Against you, you alone, have I sinned. . . .

Forgetfulness of God and the refusal to proclaim him Lord of our life are the roots of inhumanity and idolatry. And the psalm shows us how we must be totally imbued by penance to be really able to help this city.

When the Lord decided to mold us, just as the potter molds clay, he assumed a burden so heavy that he allowed his Son to be nailed to the cross so that he could fulfill the formation of pure conscience in us.

By contemplating the cross we will then be able to somewhat understand the immense burden that God takes on for us. He invites us to share this burden in order to walk patiently but clearly on the path of purification, to be apostles and prophets of our difficult cities, and to shine in the light of the Beatitudes.

3.

Sin: Betrayal of the Covenant

The Linen Loincloth

We are still in the meditations of the exercises on purification from sin.

The preceding reflection could have been summarized in the expression "Sin: Ruin of the City"; now we take a step forward toward the comprehension of sin as a betrayal of that pact of the alliance with which the Lord places—today as he did in the past—his trust in humankind and in the city.

Let us ask the grace of the Holy Spirit to enter into this deep mystery that still remains obscure to us because we do not know the heart of God well enough:

> We turn to you, Lord Jesus, who keep the mystery of the covenant deep in your heart. Grant that in contemplating you, we may be able to intuit how such a mystery implicates us and you, how it illuminates not only our external failings, but our internal relationship with you, which alone constitutes us in our true reality. Grant us that we may come to see with clear eyes the depth of this relationship, so as to love you as you want to be loved.

The prophet Jeremiah is known as the prophet of the new covenant, and we find in chapter 31 of his book one of the most quoted passages of the New Testament: "The days are surely coming, says the LORD, when I will make a new covenant with the house of Israel and the house of Judah" (v. 31). I will not stop here to comment on these words that are at the center of all Jeremiah's work (we will return to this later), because I wish to present another symbol to you, another very rich image used by the prophet: the linen loincloth. It will help us understand the biblical sense of human sinfulness.

> Thus said the LORD to me, "Go and buy yourself a linen loin-cloth, and put it on your loins, but do not dip it in water." So I bought a loincloth according to the word of the LORD, and put it on my loins. And the word of the LORD came to me a second time, saying, "Take the loincloth that you bought and are wear-ing, and go now to the Euphrates, and hide it there in a cleft of the rock." So I went and hid it by the Euphrates, as the LORD commanded me. And after many days the LORD said to me, "Go now to the Euphrates, and take from there the loincloth that I commanded you to hide there." Then I went to the Euphrates, and dug, and I took the loincloth from the place where I had hidden it. But now the loincloth was ruined; it was good for nothing.
>
> Then the word of the LORD came to me: thus says the LORD: Just so I will ruin the pride of Judah and the great pride of Jerusalem. This evil people, who refuse to hear my words, who stubbornly follow their own will and have gone after other gods to serve them and worship them, shall be like this loin-cloth, which is good for nothing. For as the loincloth clings to one's loins, so I made the whole house of Israel and the whole house of Judah cling to me, says the LORD, in order that they might be for me a people, a name, a praise, and a glory. But they would not listen (Jer 13:1-11).

This passage, that we pluck in the forest of Jeremiah's im-ages, is composed in a continuous stream and is well unified, contrary to the excerpt just previously considered, where two sources needed to be identified.

Now the source is only one, divided into two parts:

—At first there is the symbol, without explanation (vv. 1-7).

—Then there is the explanatory oracle (vv. 8-11).

Lectio of Jeremiah 13:1-11

1. Let us begin from the first seven verses, the enigmatic symbol, composed of three phrases:

> —an order (to buy the loincloth) and a carrying out ("I bought it");
> —an order (to hide the loincloth) and a carrying out ("I hid it");
> —an order (take the loincloth) and a carrying out ("I took it").

Everything unfolds in the rhythm of obedience: the prophet does not know the motive of the orders; therefore, he obeys without understanding. The loincloth, in the end, is rotten and unusable. Why does a lovely loincloth become useless?

The oracle explains it in verses 8-10. The loincloth is Judea, it's Jerusalem, my people, my city that, having adored the idols and forgotten me, is now rotten and unusable. Sin is also explained, as we reflected on it in regard to the broken jug: it is abandoning the covenant, refusing to trust in the Lord, hardness of heart, and lack of will to choose God's plan as a point of reference. Secondly, there is idolatry (he follows other gods). Missing is that aspect of inhumanity that we saw resulting from the lack of trust in the Lord and from idolatry.

Everything concludes in verse 11, which is the climax of the passage: "For as the loincloth clings to one's loins, so I made the whole house of Israel and the whole house of Judah cling to me, says the LORD, in order that they might be for me a people, a name, a praise, and a glory. But they would not listen."

Even the story of the potter's workshop ended with the words: as a potter, so I with you, and here Jeremiah's visual prophetic style can be seen. He feels just what the people feel: as they easily understand certain gestures and images, so the prophet prefers to work with these popular symbols.

This seems to me also a precious teaching for our preaching, which should be more fluid and more enriched by popular metaphors.

2. How and where should the episode of the linen loincloth and the subsequent oracle be placed?

The mention of the river would in itself indicate that it takes place in Mesopotamia, hence at the time of the deportation—at least after the first invasion of Jerusalem.

Nevertheless, the interpreters believe that the Hebrew word *peràt* does not refer to the Euphrates, because it is far from the holy city; and, furthermore, there is no other mention of any trip by the prophet to this river. They then suggest that the action took place in Wadi Farah, six kilometers north of Anothoth, in the desert zone between Jerusalem, the north, and the Jordan River. In this case the event would have to be placed at a time before the deportation. I recommend this text for your personal rereading because I feel pressed to dwell extensively on the *meditatio.*

The Teaching on the Covenant

I will explain the message of the text in a series of themes: the covenant as will of God, project of God; the covenant as a mutual acceptance of God and of humanity; the covenant as pride of God; the disappointed covenant; the new covenant, a theme connecting the two testaments; the covenant and the city.

1. Verse 11 clearly shows that the covenant, namely, the mutual adherence of the people to God and of God to the people as the loincloth around a man's hips, is God's will, his project for humanity.

The Bible gives a very simple answer to the question of what God wants from humankind; what is his wish for human history? The will of God is the covenant. This is the synthesis of all the history of humankind as God sees it; in other words, God creates men and women for a covenant.

We know the basic formula of the alliance that appears from the very first books of Scripture. For example, in Exodus 6:7: "I will take you as my people and I will be your God. . . . ["You are my people, I am your God."] Humanity is represented in the Old Testament as the people of God, in Israel. Again, in Exodus 19:5: "You shall be my treasured possession out of all the peoples, you shall be for me a priestly kingdom and a holy nation." In these few words, we see the creative and redemptive project of the Lord who works in history so as to have a people, a humanity belonging to God from the heart. We can say that the history of humankind should be the external projection of the intimate story of God: God lives in himself a mysterious, inexpressible, and most profound covenant whereby the Father is everything for the Son, the Son is everything for the Father, and this, in the Spirit, is the glory, the fullness of God. God wishes to spread forth the project that is himself; hence God constitutes in the Son a people that can be his as the Son belongs to the Father, a people to whom he can say "You are mine, and I am yours." The covenant is the very Trinity projected into history.

For this reason, the formula of the covenant runs through the whole Bible, the New and Old Testament, and is expressed, in Jeremiah, by the image of the linen loincloth.

2. The linen loincloth suggests more specifically a second reflection: the covenant is a mutual agreement. Here the mystery is expressed in physical, carnal, and almost spousal terms.

The adhesion of the loincloth to the person's body occurs in other pages of Scripture. For example, in a negative way where evil is mentioned:

> "May it be like a garment that he wraps around himself,
>   like a belt that he wears every day" (Ps 109:19).

It is something that pervades the live core of a human being in order to underline the sense of reciprocity. The theme of adhesion is especially expressed by St. Paul in a very daring passage where he compares the adherence to Christ with the physical adherence of a man to a woman, even to a prostitute:

> Do you not know that your bodies are members of Christ? Should I therefore take the members of Christ and make them

members of a prostitute? Never! Do you not know that whoever is united to a prostitute becomes one body with her? For it
is said, "The two shall be one flesh." But anyone united to the
Lord becomes one spirit with him (1 Cor 6:15-17).

It is almost a physical form of the covenant: to be one body, to
adhere almost physically to the Lord. This is the force of God's
plan.

3. This plan of God, so concrete and significant, is God's
merit, God's glory. These words of the oracle are marvelous:
"So that you would be my people, my fame, my praise and
glory."

In Hebrew, my "fame" is *shem*, "my name": I am the Lord,
you are my name. God communicates his name mysteriously,
so that the people who bear his name identify with him, are his
renown, his pride. And he concedes his own glory to his people,
he communicates it to them. The glory of God is his people,
humanity. The word "my praise," in Hebrew *tehillà*, pervades
the psalms. God is praised in his people, the people are his
praise; God looks forward to it in the end result of a well-
shaped, artistic, precious earthenware vase, an extraordinary
masterpiece: you are my praise.

My "glory," in Hebrew *tiferèt*, is that in which God prides
himself. It may be helpful, to understand the fullness of the
word *tiferèt*, to read Esther's scroll, where it is used to indicate
the great treasures of King Ahasuerus:

> . . . the nobles and governors of the province were present,
> while he displayed the great wealth of his kingdom and the
> splendor and pomp of his majesty for many days, one hundred
> eighty days in all.
>
> When these days were completed, the king gave for all the
> people present in the citadel of Susa, both great and small, a
> banquet lasting for seven days, in the court of the garden of the
> king's palace. There were white cotton curtains and blue hang-
> ings tied with cords of fine linen and purple to silver rings and
> marble pillars. There were couches of gold and silver on a mo-
> saic pavement of porphyry, marble, mother-of-pearl, and colored

stones. Drinks were served in golden goblets, goblets of different kinds, and the royal wine was lavished according to the bounty of the king (Esth 1:4-7).

The king prides himself in all of this because it gives witness to his wealth and magnanimity; it is what he is proud of, what he boasts about. God is proud; he boasts of his people. The king is happy to prepare a lavish banquet where everyone can be at ease, celebrate, and be joyous because, in this way, he shows his personal glory. God delights in our feast, our joy, our serene living, our pleasure in life, our cheerfulness. We are his glory, this is his plan, expressed with the typical concreteness of the Old Testament.

4. The bitterness and disappointment with which the Lord says the last words in Jeremiah are understandable: "But they did not listen to me."

The rotten loincloth is the unkept, uncultivated covenant that degenerates.

God is saddened by sin because humankind has not believed in his promise for happiness, has not corresponded to his covenant, his plan.

In fact, God is not simply a master who checks if a servant did or did not execute an order, a precept; he is a friend who has invested emotionally in us as his friends, as a bridegroom who has invested everything in his bride to make her glorious, beautiful, resplendent, and happy, yet feels betrayed in the end.

It is difficult for us to understand that we are God's "wealth," that he has tied himself to us to the point that our success is also his, our failure is his, our lack of communication is his disappointment, our laziness his sadness. I have been told of a Jesuit priest (whom I knew well) who died of cancer a few years ago, and who during his painful illness continued to say "Lord, I am your treasure." Not "You, my God, are my treasure," but "I am the one who is your masterpiece."

There is another text of Jeremiah that recaptures the theme of the loincloth yet reverses the terms; the loincloth is God himself for Israel considered as the bride:

Can a girl forget her ornaments,
    or a bride her attire?
Yet my people have forgotten me,
    days without number" (Jer 2:32).

God is the loincloth of Israel, he has attached himself to it, feeling a bitter disappointment when he realizes that the people do not take pride in such a loincloth.

5. If then God is touched by humanity's response and by the city's negative answer, we can ask ourselves: Why is it a matter of a *new* covenant? Because God does not stay disappointed forever, does not accept his treasure being lost, hence he makes a new covenant.

Jeremiah, who witnesses the loss of God's plan and God's deep bitterness for the city of Jerusalem, is the one who foresees the coming of a new covenant, the alliance that will be fully realized in Jesus: "This cup that is poured out for you is the new covenant of my blood" (Luke 22:20), but the prophet then announces: "The days are surely coming, says the LORD, when I will make a new covenant with the house of Israel and the house of Judah" (Jer 31:31).

Jesus takes upon himself the consequences of God's disappointment and frustration in his plan in order to give us back to him.

So, in essence, the rebuilding of the covenant that we hold every day in our hands in the Eucharist is already present in the image of the linen loincloth. When we pronounce the words of Jesus over the chalice, we remember the whole mystery: the first covenant, sin, the betrayal of the covenant, God's bitterness, and Jesus, who dies on the cross bearing God's disappointment just in order to rebuild the covenant.

6. The last reflection is on the relationship between the covenant and the city.

—God really loves our cities, he loves the city made up by humanity; he wants it to be his, as a part of himself, as a belt around his body, as his glory, his name. And he is saddened, he weeps over the city when it does not respond, when it has become a rotten loincloth.

Jesus suffers and dies to take on all the evils, the contradictions, the wickedness of the city. And we too, priests and bishops, must take upon us the contradictions, the poverty, the misery, the marginalization, the cries and pain of humanity, then place them in the chalice and in the host at Mass. Hence the Eucharist is the very heart of the city's redemption, and as long as a city—be it even Sodom or Gomorrah—celebrates the Eucharist, we have nothing to fear because the life of the city is continuously renewed in the Eucharist. Now we can have a glimpse of understanding for a pastoral and apostolic vocation that mysteriously takes part in the atoning and redemptive action of the Son of God.

But the story of the city and of humanity is also my personal story because I am the loincloth of God. With baptism, God has placed me around himself, has gambled everything on me, in Jesus. So every response on my part that is weak, lukewarm, deaf, or negligent, represents a failure for him.

From this we can gain a real sense of what our sins, our lack of response, truly are: they prevent the divine design to reach his planned result of glory; they keep God from manifesting in me the fullness of his love.

Toward *Contemplatio*

Just as we are being introduced to contemplation, it is useful for each of us to rethink our view of our interpersonal relationship with God.

Do I feel that the covenant with God, as shown by the linen loincloth, is touching me urgently, is my fate, my destiny?

If this covenant is not cultivated, it rots to harm me; I cannot simply lock it up in a safe, but I must hold it tight against me.

When and how do I feel I am neglecting it?

The relationship with God must be understood in terms of a deep friendship, a design much grander than the one expressed in the moral law or in the formal observance of the commandments. It is a relationship that involves me in the totality of the plan in which the Lord gives himself to me.

> Grant, O Father, that I may so well understand your plan of love for me as to desire suffering with Jesus for my failings and those of my brothers and sisters. Grant that I may place myself in your hands as in the hands of the potter, that I may tightly hold the loincloth to my hips with gratitude and humility.

4.

The Wine-jar

Help us, Lord, to deeply experience the mystery of purification. Be the one to purify our hearts and allow us to understand the mystery of your wrath.

Today most of us fear using the expression "Wrath of God," yet, we should try to understand the meaning of the word that frightens us and that we have purposely removed from our ways of speaking.

Let us, therefore, try to finish the meditation on purifying the heart by reading (among many possible choices) three passages of Jeremiah as an introduction to others that offer precious images, and that I personally invite you to read. Jeremiah, in fact, is not only a poet who uses symbols and allusions; he is also a painter who chooses as subjects of his canvases the different moments of existence, the events of daily life.

I have chosen three small canvases in which he reflects, starting with concrete circumstances: a jar of wine, darkness and light (night that is approaching), and the scarecrows. These are three images used by Jeremiah to indicate the theme of the wrath of God that is his very own.

The Wine-jar

After the narration of the linen loincloth, and almost as a way of continuing, we find the story of the wine-jar that was usually seen, even on the table of the poor.

You shall speak to them this word: Thus says the LORD, the God of Israel: Every wine-jar should be filled with wine. And they will say to you, "Do you think we do not know that every wine-jar should be filled with wine?" Then you shall say to them: Thus says the LORD: "I am about to fill all the inhabitants of this land—the kings who sit on David's throne, the priests, the prophets, and all the inhabitants of Jerusalem—with drunkenness. And I will dash them one against another, parents and children together, says the LORD. I will not pity or spare or have compassion when I destroy them" (Jer 13:12-14).

It is a terrible oracle, harsh and gripping.

Lectio of Jeremiah 13:12-14

In order to reread the passage, we will divide it into two parts.

1. The first part (v. 12) is mysterious, enigmatic (every jug must be filled with wine), and elicits a question on the part of the listeners: What does it mean?

2. The second part (v. 13-14) is composed of the oracle itself: "I am about to fill all the inhabitants of this land with drunkenness."

It is a question of a double punishment; the one of drunkenness, and the one of destruction of the people ("I will dash them one against another").

The passage hints at the punishment for the broken covenant. In the preceding meditation we witnessed the shame of the broken alliance in a rotten, unusable belt: the people become useless.

Now we see the negative effects; not only the fading of a nation, but punishments as well. Drunkenness, whereby people become mad, irresponsible, dazed, and unable to guide themselves, is the image of a people who has lost all sense of orientation, of values, of just things, and of truth. The image of individuals being dashed against the other underlines how a society self-destructs by losing its values.

Negativity and disloyalty to the alliance produce the total destruction of a society. Jeremiah is particularly interested in social themes; he fights for a just, flourishing, peaceful, and harmonious city in which all individuals can have the best for their development. He feels deeply saddened when he realizes that Jerusalem fails to attain a level of orientation, of cohesion, and of unity while its inhabitants mutually destroy each other. This is the drama of Jeremiah's life: he constantly notices a city on the way to decay, he warns it with an invitation to change, yet no one listens to his words.

—On this subject, it is useful here to remember chapter 25 (v. 15-38), which prepares for the final chapters of the book, where the prophet resumes the theme of drunkenness as a punishment (we will see the references in the New Testament). Until now everything we have read of Jeremiah was directed to the holy city; even the other nations, however, have sinned by abandoning the covenant, and have therefore fallen into God's wrath. Now we are facing a series of oracles against the pagan nations, which in the Hebrew text are placed in chapters 46–51, while in the Greek version (LXX) we find them placed right after chapter 25. The image of drunkenness applies to all nations.

We read a few verses:

> For thus the LORD, the God of Israel, said to me: Take from my hand this cup of the wine of wrath, and make all the nations to whom I send you drink it. They shall drink and stagger and go out of their minds because of the sword that I am sending among them.
>
> So I took the cup from the LORD's hand, and made all the nations to whom the LORD sent me drink it: Jerusalem and the towns of Judah, its kings and officials, to make them a desolation and a waste, an object of hissing and of cursing, as they are today; Pharaoh king of Egypt, his servants, his officials, and all his people; all the mixed people; all the kings of the land of Uz; all the kings of the land of the Philistines—Ashkelon, Gaza,

Ekron and the remnant of Ashdod; Edom, Moab and the
Ammonites; all the kings of Tyre, all the kings of Sidon, and the
kings of the coast land across the sea; Dedan, Tema, Buz, and
all who have shaven temples; all the kings of Arabia and all the
kings of the mixed peoples that live in the desert; all the kings
of Zimri, all the kings of Elam, and all the kings of Media; all
the kings of the north, far and near, one after another, and all
the kingdoms of the world that are on the face of the earth. And
after them the king of Sheshach shall drink (Jer 25:15-26) . . .

namely, to all the nations against which the oracles will be proclaimed from chapter 46 on.

The symbol of the cup of God's wrath that produces
drunkenness in evil persons and makes them lose their minds,
becoming spiritually fragmented, shows precisely how God
punishes those who have denied the covenant, like Israel, or
whoever has not recognized the Lord of history, like the pagan
nations.

I would like to note that in speaking of the cup of wrath
against Jerusalem, the prophet is referring to the responsible
individuals, those who have a civic or religious function; he is
not making reference to the people: "the kings who sit on
David's throne, the priests, the prophets and all the inhabitants of Jerusalem" (Jer 13:13).

And in 25:15: "Jerusalem and the towns of Judah, its kings
and officials, to make them a desolation and a waste, an object
of hissing and of cussing":

The notion that the people fall through the fault of kings
and priests is very strong in Jeremiah. The people suffer, will
have to go into exile, yet it is really the civic and religious authorities who carry the greatest responsibility for the disasters.
It is not by chance that Jeremiah's prophecy was so opposed
by the authorities while it was well-liked by the people.

Meditatio on God's Wrath

What does "Wrath of God" mean?

1. We instinctively refuse to think that God becomes angry and punishes his creatures, that he sends people into exile, that he causes famine and destruction. It seems to us that to attribute punishment to God is typical of a past era when God was considered the origin of everything, both good and evil. I believe that today, with the best of intentions, we prefer not to speak of an external wrath of God, as if he intervenes from the outside to punish, but rather of an imminent wrath in the sense that by abandoning the alliance, the people lose their sense of values, hence decline, and the punishment is then imminent to the loss of the covenant. In other words, humanity is itself preparing a punishment with its own hands.

If the covenant means happiness, then the loss of this covenant is equal to unhappiness, just as in the New Testament Jesus juxtaposes the Beatitudes to "woes" (cf. Luke 6:20-26), underlining a happiness tied to the covenant and an unhappiness stemming from the abandonment of it.

Such an interpretation seems to me legitimate, given that the Lord has connected the welfare of the people and of each one of us to the observance of his covenant, in the "abiding" in his love, in seeking his will. If and when we detach from this will, we slowly plunge into unhappiness, boredom, disgust of life, and into the impossibility of finding our way.

2. Nevertheless, a notion of imminent justice, whereby sin creates in a human being that lack of meaning that leads to sadness and unhappiness, does not grasp the total mystery of God's wrath. Should we then turn to the notion of a vindictive God who personally throws his bolts of angry lightning against sinners?

I think there is a third way, which is the one reflecting the saving wrath of God, expressed in the gospel in regard to Jesus. We have already recalled that he resumes some of Jeremiah's speeches against Jerusalem. For example, in rereading Luke 21:10: "Nation will rise against nation, and kingdom against kingdom . . ." we find Jesus expressing in other terms the word: "I will dash one against the other," namely, the internal fragmentation of the people and of the nations.

There is, however, a verse of the Gospel according to John that allows us a deeper understanding of the mystery, and that is also a decisive word for our path of interior purification: John 18:11, the beginning of the Passion. Jesus is about to be arrested in the Garden of Olives and Peter, with the force of his ardor, hits the servant of the high priest with his sword and cuts off his right ear. Then Jesus says to Peter: "Put your sword back in the sheath. Am I not to drink the cup that the Father has given me?" The cup of God's wrath that Jeremiah talks about, and that is the inherent punishment for all human evil, is drunk by Jesus. This is the mystery of redemption, of the re-establishment of the covenant: that Jesus himself comes to drink the cup of the wrath of God, assuming upon himself our sin (cf. 2 Cor 5:21), in order to rebuild God's plan. Jesus, in the name of humanity, takes upon himself God's wrath, well justified by our sins, that inherent wrath that is the injustice in the world. Jesus does not submit himself to an external wrath of God, as if the Father wished to punish the Son, rather he drinks the cup of the world's injustice, hence becoming redeemer of humanity and mediator of the new covenant.

This is the mystery of the Cross, and without a constant and loving contemplation of the crucifix, we will not be able to adequately interpret the words on wrath, the foreshadowing of disasters, and the threats pronounced by Jeremiah, by other Old Testament prophets and by Jesus. It is God himself who, in his Son, allows himself to be crushed by the consequences of sin by fulfilling the greatest wrath and the greatest mercy. It is a mystery born out of the Trinity. Theologians today try to delve more deeply into the trinitarian mystery, and, in the last ten years, much has been written on this topic. In their studies, I am impressed by the attempt to already seek in the Trinity the roots of the Cross.

Hence, the Cross does not seem like an event extrinsic to God, a fortuitous event that by chance happens to Jesus. It is, instead, part of the mystery of the covenant, the mystery of God who so deeply makes an alliance with the rotten loincloth as to accept upon himself the very rotting of the cloth in order to redeem humanity.

All this is not only an act of Jesus, but also part of the mystery of divine giving: God gives himself to such an extent, he so much fills humankind with himself that he takes on even sin and the wrath of such sin.

We will never be able to fully understand this mystery, yet in the Eucharist we hold it in our hands; it is the mystery whereby the divinity burdens itself with the injustice of the world, to then redeem it through self-giving. And we could say that it is the deepest level of true liberation theology.

I believe that every theology of redemption must always have at its center the image of God in the Trinity who fights human injustice on the cross by giving back to humanity the possibility of building a free, peaceful, and holy people.

Light and Darkness: Jeremiah 13:15-17

In the familiar image of the wine-jar, we have perceived something of the mystery of redemption, and now we see an exhortative oracle in which Jeremiah repeats, in various ways, the same concept. In fact, he continues to proclaim only one prophecy: sin is the ruin of a people, and God prepares the resurrection of this people.

Jeremiah 13:15-17: "Hear and give ear; do not be haughty, for the LORD has spoken. Give glory to the LORD your God before he brings darkness, and before your feet stumble on the mountains at twilight"; (vv. 15-16a and b)—therefore, convert before night falls—"while you look for light, he turns it into gloom and makes it deep darkness" (v. 16c). This verse is a judgment of retaliation: if you have faith in the light of your pride, I will be darkness for you.

Verse 17, which gives witness to the particular sensitivity of the prophet, is very significant:

> But if you will not listen,
>   my soul will weep in secret for your pride;
> my eyes will weep bitterly and run down with tears,
>   because the LORD's flock has been taken captive.

It is again a metaphor of God's judgment: those who thought they possessed the light have been trapped in darkness; the secular city, sure of itself, of its technical discoveries, of its own sociology and political organization, has gradually entered into the darkness. And the prophet weeps.

Again, recalling the gospel, especially that of Luke's, who, among the evangelists, best reflects Jeremiah's spirit:

> As he came near and saw the city, he wept over it, saying, "If you, even you, had only recognized on this day the things that make for peace! But now they are hidden from your eyes. Indeed, the days will come upon you, when your enemies will set up ramparts around you and surround you, and hem you in on every side. They will crush you to the ground, you and your children within you, and they will not leave within you one stone upon another; because you did not recognize the time of your visitation from God (Luke 19:41-44).

This is a typical word of Jeremiah, transposed in Luke's gospel. Jeremiah weeps secretly, to the point of having no tears left; and on the basis of this crying that will even run out of tears, the Book of Lamentations will return, inspired by our prophet to speak of the fall of Jerusalem.

Meditatio on the Weeping of Jeremiah and of Jesus

Crying signifies the prophet's personal participation in the suffering of his people. Jeremiah does not accuse from afar but becomes totally involved, living in the drama of the people; he is not a simple ambassador who retires under diplomatic immunity after having given out his message. He is a man who suffers when he speaks, and for what he must announce. In this respect, he is the image of Jesus who cries over the city, alerts it to what will soon happen to it, yet he will be the first one to die for the city. The greatest prophecy of Jesus on Jerusalem will be his death.

We are now in front of a large painting in which we see ourselves as persons called in some way to be prophets of the

New Testament; not to accuse society, to complain about it as if it were far from us, but rather to become involved in its difficulties and dramas, in its sufferings and in its problems.

It is our suffering that saves society, humanity; it is the cry of Jesus that is a redeeming one for the city of Jerusalem. And when we think of our sins as negative realities that have made the Church less faithful, less luminous and resplendent, we become involved in the purification of the people, and we learn to weep mostly for ourselves, so as to become able to weep with Jesus for our cities.

The Scarecrows: Jeremiah 10:1-16

I have found in Jeremiah 10:1-16 a last image suggesting reflection on the theme of redemption.

> Hear the word that the LORD speaks to you, O house of Israel. Thus says the LORD:
> Do not learn the way of the nations,
> or be dismayed at the signs of the heavens;
> for the nations are dismayed at them.
> For the customs of the people are false:
> a tree from the forest is cut down,
> and worked with an ax by the hands of an artisan;
> people deck it with silver and gold;
> they fasten it with hammer and nails
> so that it cannot move.
> Their idols are like scarecrows in a cucumber field,
> and they cannot speak;
> they have to be carried, for they cannot walk.
> Do not be afraid of them, for they cannot do evil,
> nor is it in them to do good.
>
> There is none like you, O LORD;
> you are great, and your name is great in might.
> Who would not fear you, O King of the nations?
> For that is your due;
> among all the wise ones of the nations

and in all their kingdoms there is no one like you.
They are both stupid and foolish;
    the instruction given by idols is no better than wood!
Beaten silver is brought from Tarshish,
    and gold from Uphaz.
They are the work of the artisan and of the hands of the
        goldsmith;
    their clothing is blue and purple;
    they are all the product of skilled workers.
But the LORD is the true God;
    he is the living God and the everlasting King.
At his wrath the earth quakes, and the nations cannot endure
        his indignation.

Thus shall you say to them: The gods who did not make the heavens and the earth shall perish from the earth and from under the heavens.

It is he who made the earth by his power,
    who established the world by his wisdom,
    and by his understanding stretched out the heavens.
When he utters his voice, there is a tumult of waters in the
        heavens,
    and he makes the mist rise from the ends of the earth.
He makes lightnings for the rain,
    and he brings out the wind from his storehouses.
Everyone is stupid and without knowledge;
    goldsmiths are all put to shame by their idols;
for their images are false, and there is no breath in them.
They are worthless, a work of delusion;
    at the time of their punishment they shall perish.
Not like these is the LORD, the portion of Jacob,
    for he is the one who formed all things,
and Israel is the tribe of his inheritance;
    the LORD of hosts is his name (Jer 10:1-16).

We have read a message against idolatry, one of the three components of the breakdown of the covenant (indifference in regard to the Lord or forgetting Him, idolatry, and inhumanity).

Jeremiah says to the people: the idols representing human passions are nothing, and we must not fear their strength. Translating for us, the idols of our modern cities are sensuality, money, power, idols transmitted through the mass media, that are fed by political skirmishes and seem to dominate the city. Do not fear them, because when you look at them in the face and confront them directly, you will notice that they have no power. Their appearance produces fear, but in fact we must laugh at them.

It is the strength of the gospel and of the Beatitudes that silences its idols, juxtaposing to them the victorious strength of the humility and weakness of Jesus. We will speak of this later, when attempting to capture the positive aspect of our experience, namely, the calling to be imbued, in God's covenant, with the same strength as Jesus.

In the meantime, let us ask the Lord to help us fulfill well the sacrament of confession, living it as a sacrament of the covenant. Confession before being a *confessio vitae*, a recognition of my sins, must be a *confessio laudis*, a proclamation of the gifts and marvels of God (how great you are in me, Lord God of the covenant! How many gifts you have given me!) In front of such gifts even my betrayals of the covenant take on a more painful and true light, filling me with trust.

Then confession will not just be a routine that at the end does not produce change, but an event marking the Lord's mercy that transforms my life, a dialogue that begins with the experience of the mystery of the covenant and then reforms me.

HOMILY

Tuesday of the Eighteenth Week in Ordinary Time, Cycle I

Contemplating the Face of Jesus

Today's liturgy offers us two readings very rich in instruction for us and our retreat, but I will limit myself to just a few comments.

Looking at Jesus

—In the passage of Matthew's gospel (Matt 14:22-36), we see the beautiful image of Jesus who ". . . went up to the mountain by himself to pray. When evening came, he was there alone. . . ." Through the ages, all the great masters of prayer were inspired by this image, as were the monks who hold vigils during the night, so we too will be inspired by it.

Certainly just as we pray on the mount represented by this House for Spiritual Exercises, in many parts of the world and even in our community it is night and there are storms. Yet if we persevere with the Lord in the silence of prayer, we are united to all through the very prayer of Jesus.

—The second part of Matthew's story lends itself to being read in a rather ecclesiastical tone. Jesus, having come down from the mount, reaches his disciples, who are now in the boat, by walking on the water; Peter would like to go to him over the water, but despite Jesus' invitation, he is frightened by the vehemence of the wind and fears drowning, hence the Lord reprimands him. All this means that Jesus gives courage to his Church, allowing it to go through trials and storms, yet not wanting it to feel fearful. So he addresses the Church through Peter, who is the symbol of courage and of the trials of this Church.

The gospels, in fact, are not afraid to have us see, besides courage, also difficulty, weakness, and the fragility of Peter so that the Church can feel more close to him and more represented by him both in courage and in toil. He is part of the Church and we are called to live in unity with him as we all look together to the Lord.

When Peter begins to walk on the waters, his eyes, as are those of his disciples, are fixed on Jesus, but just at the moment when he stops looking at him, he weakens: ". . . when he noticed the strong wind, he became frightened, and beginning to sink, he cried out: Lord, save me!"

Noticeable is the fact that the Greek text offers a more precise reading: not "because of the strong wind," but "seeing the strong wind." It means that Peter was looking at the wind, not at Jesus, hence he becomes frightened.

We, therefore, ask the Lord that we may never divert our gaze from Him, especially when we are frightened by trials, anxieties, and difficulties, because only from contemplating his divine face can we obtain the courage to persevere.

Humility and Meekness of Moses

The first reading (Num 12:1-13) is also very important from an ecclesiastical point of view because it describes an internal dialectical process occurring within the three great responsible persons in the people of Israel: Miriam, Aaron, and Moses. We could not have imagined that there could be any problems or difficulties among them.

Moses, with all his charisma, does not escape certain criticisms that seem justified in our passage: ". . . Miriam and Aaron spoke against Moses because of the Cushite woman whom he had married. . . ." Perhaps in that time laws strictly excluding marriage between the Jews and persons of other tribes were not yet in effect, but in any case he had not acted meritoriously by taking a wife from a different country.

Yet the Lord defends him. It seems rather strange that in this page of Numbers, Moses is described as being ". . . very humble, more so than anyone else on the face of the earth." He was not, in fact, humble, but a strong, rough man capable of shouting and yelling at the people in order to shake and stimulate them.

Why then is he called "very humble?" Probably because in the context of the passage he does not react to the criticism of his brothers, although the criticisms were unexpected and hurt him deeply. On other occasions, instead, he did react, but these were criticisms that could damage the honor of God.

> [And the LORD said to Miriam and Aaron]:
> "Not so with my servant Moses;
>
> he is entrusted with all my house.
> With him I speak face to face—clearly, not in riddles;
>
> and he beholds the form of the LORD.
> Why then were you not afraid to speak against my servant Moses?" (Num 12:7-8).

Hence, he was a strong man, also humble and meek (of that kind of humility that Jesus encourages us to have: "Take my yoke upon you, and learn from me; for I am gentle and humble in heart . . ." (Matt 11:29); because of this humility and meekness, God goes to his defense.

—Furthermore, I would like to suggest that you reflect on the relationship of the prayer of Moses with God that, in some way, completes the image of Jesus praying on the mount. If we ask ourselves how Jesus prayed on the mount, we could actually answer with the recently quoted expression: Jesus spoke face to face with God, clearly and not in riddles, and he beheld the face of the Father.

"To speak face to face" recalls the instruction of St. Ignatius of Loyola in his booklet of *Spiritual Exercises* regarding meditations: "To speak to God as a friend speaks to a friend" (m. 54), and we are invited to pursue this sort of dialogue both during the Eucharist and in other moments of prayer.

5.

The Memory of the Vocation

The Image of Jeremiah

We have by now evoked a number of images of Jeremiah's preaching: the potter's shop, the broken jug, the linen loincloth, the wine-jar, darkness and light, and the scarecrows. These rich symbols have helped us on the path of purification and belong to the prophet's moral preaching that in turn touches our moral life and that of the people, a preaching that aims to make us understand the expectations of the covenant.

Even the speech in the temple, in chapter 7, is to be read as a synthesis of these demands.

It needs to be said, though, that among the remembered images and the very numerous other ones that each of you will find when reading the book, the strongest and most extraordinary image of the mystery of God in history is Jeremiah; he is preaching itself, his whole life is prophecy. We, therefore, wish to turn more directly to the contemplation of his person. Who was this man who spoke with such fervor, with so much participation and strength?

We will answer this question by starting from the basic text in which he expressed his self-knowledge, the rock on which he based his very existence. If we had asked Jeremiah: Why do you behave so? Why do you preach in this way? Why do you suffer so much? He would simply have answered: because God has called me. His vocation is the constant force that sustains him through trials and disappointments.

I have, therefore, chosen a passage from chapter 1, that we could call the memory of vocation; it is not really a story in the immediate present, but one written by the prophet many years later. This shows how deeply engraved in him was the word that the Lord directed toward him when he was eighteen years old.

It is a splendid and very well-known excerpt and we will reflect on it according to the traditional divisions; we will reread it so as to grasp the important elements it contains; we will reflect on the message; finally, for the *contemplatio*, I will suggest that we pray facing God, each of us bringing to mind his own calling, and rebuilding it as rock and foundation of our lives.

> Now the word of the LORD came to me saying,
>> "Before I formed you in the womb I knew you,
>> and before you were born I consecrated you;
>> I appointed you a prophet to the nations."
>
> Then I said, "Ah, Lord GOD! Truly I do not know how to speak,
> for I am only a boy." But the LORD said to me,
>> "Do not say, 'I am only a boy';
>> for you shall go to all to whom I send you,
>> and you shall speak whatever I command you,
>> Do not be afraid of them,
>> for I am with you to deliver you, says the LORD."
>
> Then the LORD put out his hand and touched my mouth; and
> the LORD said to me,
>> "Now I have put my words in your mouth.
>> See, today I appoint you over nations and over kingdoms,
>> to pluck up and to pull down,
>> to destroy and to overthrow,
>> to build and to plant."
>
> The word of the LORD came to me, saying, "Jeremiah, what do
> you see?" And I said, "I see a branch of an almond tree." Then
> the LORD said to me, "You have seen well, for I am watching
> over my word to perform it." The word of the LORD came to me
> a second time, saying, "What do you see?" And I said, "I see a
> boiling pot, tilted away from the north."
>
> The LORD said to me: Out of the north disaster shall break
> out on all the inhabitants of the land. For now I am calling all

the tribes of the kingdoms of the north, says the LORD; and they shall come and all of them shall set their thrones at the entrance of the gates of Jerusalem, against all its surrounding walls and against all the cities of Judah. And I will utter my judgments against them, for all their wickedness in forsaking me; they have made offerings to other gods, and worshiped the works of their own hands. But you, gird up your loins; stand up and tell them everything that I command you. Do not break down before them or I will break you before them. And I for my part have made you today a fortified city, an iron pillar, and a bronze wall, against the whole land—against the kings of Judah, its princes, its priests, and the people of the land. They will fight against you; but they shall not prevail against you, for I am with you, says the LORD, to deliver you (Jer 1:4-19).

This text is particularly dense with references or recollections of other passages of Scripture, while numerous verses of both the Old and the New Testaments refer to this passage of Jeremiah. It can certainly stimulate us to awaken our personal insight into our vocation and mission.

Grant us, O Lord, that remembering your gifts and the calling of Jeremiah the prophet, we may penetrate more deeply into the awareness of our calling and learn to inscribe it in our memory as a defense and support for the future.

Lectio of Jeremiah 1:4-19

A. Understanding the structure of a passage may seem to be an academic exercise, but I find it essential to understand the message.

The exegetes have suggested many divisions in the text that are valid but not all satisfactory, at least regarding the path of our exercises. I would, therefore, like to offer you one of my suggestions.

1. First of all, I pick a fundamental and substantive word or phrase that I summarize, such as "Forever I have called you."

We read, in fact: "Before I formed you in the womb I knew you, / and before you were born I consecrated you; / I appointed you a prophet to the nations" (v. 5).

Three verses, almost as a poem, that repeat the same concept: you have always been mine, in order to be called.

—After this component word, there follows one of resistance: "Ah, Lord GOD! Truly I do not know how to speak, for I am only a boy" (v. 6).

But the Lord reconfirms: "Go to all to whom I send you and you shall speak whatever I command you" (v. 7).

This is the vocation that Jeremiah felt vibrating in him, as an existential call.

This word is immediately made specific with a symbolic gesture: "And the LORD said to me: now I have put my words in your mouth" (v. 9).

—Then comes an oracle that again takes up the notion of mission: "See, today I appoint you over nations and over kingdoms, to pluck up and pull down, to destroy and to overthrow, to build and to plant" (v. 10). The substance of the vocation is completely enclosed in verses 4-10.

2. From verses 11 to 19, four symbols and four oracles are described that give rhythm to the explanation of Jeremiah's mission with a very precise structure: a symbol and an oracle; a symbol and an oracle; a symbol and an oracle; a symbol and an oracle. Hence, we notice that the passage is composed with great care.

—The first symbol is that of the almond tree branch, and the oracle assures Jeremiah that God is watching over him.

—The second is the symbol of the cauldron on the fire, and the oracle affirms that disaster will pour forth from the north.

—The third symbol is about girding one's loins and standing upright, while the oracle repeats not to be afraid or frightened.

—The last symbol is one of strength, the bronze wall, and the oracle warns that Jeremiah will never be conquered because the Lord is with him.

It is important to observe that the prophet never speaks without symbols and gestures that make the word of God concrete; also in this first chapter there is already a series of elements creating the notion of an event full of consequences for Jeremiah's life and for his social and political influence. Kings, peoples, Israel, and the pagans are quoted, namely the whole historic and geographical framework of his action: the suffering that he will have to endure is remembered, as well as his many difficulties and the strength that the Lord will give him against the enemies.

B. When Was the Text Written?

—It surely expresses a thought-out experience, not the original one. But we always read the precise date of this event of Jeremiah's life in chapter 1: "In the days of King Josiah son of Amon of Judah, in the thirteenth year of his reign" (v. 2) therefore around the year 627 B.C.

The age of the prophet is not indicated, but one can deduce from the affirmation "I am young," that he was between 18 and 20 years of age, when he was not yet a man capable of speaking with authority.

If we then determine Jeremiah's birth date to be in 645, this means that he had this life-changing experience, in about 627. Yet nothing is known of the previous years. Son of a priestly family probably fallen in status because his forefathers had been opposed to the kings of Jerusalem and had consequently been exiled, Jeremiah lived in Anathoth, outside of the holy city. We can assume that he was educated to know well the religion of his fathers, but we know nothing more of his infancy and adolescence.

In conclusion, he received his vocation in 647 B.C., around the age of 18.

—But we must still answer the question that we asked ourselves: when was chapter 1 written?

According to the interpreters, at least twenty years after the event happened. The occasion of the first draft is perhaps described in chapter 25, where the prophet remembers his vocation, saying to the people of Jerusalem: "For twenty-three years, from the thirteenth year of King Josiah son of Amon of Judah, to this day, the word of the LORD has come to me, and I have spoken persistently to you, but you have not listened" (v. 3). And in chapter 36: "In the fourth year . . ." (v. 1). (We are in the same fourth year of Joachim of which, in chapter 25, the prophet had said: ". . . today it is twenty-three years that I preach in vain.") "Take a writing scroll and . . ." (v. 2). The date of the writing of this oracle is 604; therefore, from 627, a bit more than twenty years have passed.

Jeremiah is living a moment of great suffering in which he realizes the total failure of his mission (he has spoken and prophesied uselessly for twenty-three years), and suddenly he feels a divine inspiration to recall the memory of the original grace, in order to gain from it the strength against disappointments. We can say that the story of chapter 1 springs from the will to endure by remembering that, despite everything, it is God who has called him, and, personally, he has done nothing more than obey the voice.

It is a highly dramatic passage, not written by a young man full of enthusiasm for his encounter with the word, full of dreams for the mission he will have to accomplish, but by a disappointed man who has experienced many failures, yet has been loyal to his initial vocation.

A Triple *Meditatio*

1. In order to look for the message of the individual moments of the passage taken from chapter 1, we will first of all work on an analytical *meditatio.*

Let us recall the fundamental message: "Before I formed you in the womb I knew you" (v. 5).

—First of all, I want to emphasize that it is a matter of a word. For Isaiah, instead, vocation corresponds to a great vision: he sees the Lord seated on a throne, and the seraphim in the temple proclaiming, "Holy, holy, holy is the LORD of the armies" (Isa 6:1-3). A glorious vision.

Even for Ezekiel, the origin of everything is a vision, the one depicting the chariot of the glory of the Lord who abandons Jerusalem (cf. Ezek 1:1ff).

Jeremiah receives a word that gives a characteristic of interiority to the prophet's vocation. It is not an external and grandiose fact, not a vision of light, but rather an internal word, as the experience of God on Mount Horeb was for Elijah: not in the wind, not in the earthquake, not in thunder—but in the whispering of a light breeze.

In this sense Jeremiah is very close to us. At least, for many of us, our vocation manifested itself as an interior voice that little by little said something to us. In this regard I like to recall that "murmur of a light wind," is translated by Hebrew scholars with the phrase "a thin voice of silence." It is in silence that God reveals himself and speaks, and Jeremiah is the man of the word that is light, subtle and listened to.

—And how does he respond to his vocation? With the sense of his inadequacy. "Ah, Lord GOD! Truly I do not know how to speak, for I am only a boy" (v. 6). It is a real inadequacy, not merely an excuse, since he was eighteen years old and had around him very authoritative adults.

—But the Lord insists: the initiative is mine, I am the one who decides. It may have occurred to Jeremiah that, for instance, in Moses' times many men were more verbal than he, not stutterers, yet God had chosen him; and that in Amos' time, there were wise men, but God had chosen him, poor shepherd and gatherer of sycamores.

In Moses, Amos, and Jeremiah, God shows that he is the one to call them and give mandates to them. The authority comes from the Lord, not from human capacity and expertise.

—The consecration is described in verse 9. The extension and imposition of hands is the gesture that marks the transmission of power. But Jeremiah's head is not touched (as today for priests and bishops) but rather his mouth: "I put my words on your mouth." Jeremiah, in fact, will not reign over a people or preside over a community, nor will he be a priest, despite his priestly family of origin; he will simply be a prophet. The gift given to him is that of the word, and in this mission he will know his limits and the power of God.

—The program of the mission entrusted to him by God is an awesome one: "See, today I appoint you over nations and over kingdoms, to pluck up and pull down, to destroy and to overthrow, to build and to plant" (v. 10).

Six verbs, four negative and two positive, indicate that the mission will be one of criticism, of threat, even if the constructive mission will be present; it will be a difficult and heavy trial.

Every prophet has his inspirational vein for his mission, his line. For instance, Deutero-Isaiah is a consoling prophet: "Console, console my people," while Jeremiah must prophesy disasters. It is not up to us to decide, but God decides each individual's mission following historical circumstances. Perhaps in our lives we will have at certain times a mission of consolation and at others a mission of threat. What most counts is to trust God, who alone calls and sends forth.

—One last important observation. It is true that Jeremiah remains as a symbol of the prophets of doom, yet he must prophesy disasters in order to sustain faith in God, who holds in his hands the unfortunate vicissitudes of the people. He is called to announce that even in disaster God holds in his hands the destiny of a people. Hence, the prophet is not called to console, saying perhaps that everything will go well, but rather to reassure that even through suffering the Lord realizes his historic design: God is the Lord of history. In this is his greatness, his capacity to preach disaster without creating discomfort or pessimism.

In this regard, there is a very interesting verse of Isaiah in a passage where, perhaps through the insistence of his disciples, he allows himself to make a personal disclosure. He is the prophet of majesty, of sanctity, who does not become emotionally involved. Nevertheless, in chapter 8, he explains the motives of his actions, of his decision to go against the public opinion of his time: "For the LORD spoke thus to me while his hand was strong upon me, and warned me not to walk in the way of this people" (Isa 8:11). And when the disciples ask him why his words are harsh, Isaiah answers: "Bind up the testimony, seal the teaching among my disciples. I will wait for the LORD, who is hiding his face from the house of Jacob, and I will hope in him" (Isa 8:16-17).

Notice the contradictions: I look at the Lord and in the moment when he diverts his glances from Jacob, namely, just when a tragedy falls on the house of Jacob, then I hope in him, I hope that he is taking care of Jacob.

Seen in this light, Jeremiah's great mission is that of the person who in any difficult situation, whether personal, familial, pastoral, civic, social or religious, believes and proclaims that it did not occur because the Lord forgot that person, but rather because he remembered him or her. Then it becomes a word of consolation.

In verse 17 a word of the Lord already underlined in verse 7 is repeated: "Tell them all that I will command you." It is very important because it lets us understand that the prophet is thrown into darkness, although a plan is given to him. He doesn't know what he will have to say from one moment to the next. A bit like Abraham, to whom it is said: "Go from your country and your kindred and your father's house to the land that I will show you" (Gen 12:1). He doesn't know where he will go, the verb is always in the future. Vocation here is not a reassuring illumination, rather a request to let go completely, to trust in the Lord.

I leave it up to you to analyze the other verses of chapter 1, so that you may enjoy them in the entire context of Jeremiah's message, while I suggest a second meditative reflection.

2. Synthetic *meditatio*. In the moment of the analytical *meditatio*, we reread certain key words found in this excerpt from the Book of Jeremiah.

Now we want to understand what experiences the prophet underwent in his vocation; among many, I will recall seven of them.

—First of all, he experiences being forever in the hands of God.

—Although he wielded no influence at his young age, he

experiences being called to a universal mission: he is sent to kings and to peoples; his life's horizon is expanded.

—He experiences his personal limits: inadequacy, impotence, fear.

—But he realizes that such limits can be overcome when one trusts in God: "You will go where I will send you."

—He experiences the strength of God in his weakness: God puts words on his lips, gives him eyes to see the true meaning of the events, and makes him like a wall of bronze.

—For the first time, he lives the experience of discernment: he sees an almond tree in bloom, he sees a cauldron, and reads in these symbols a message from God. He realizes that his capacity to interpret has been reinforced, that God is at work in history.

—Finally, he realizes that in his weak, frail, timid being, something has changed; there is a new nature in him, a strength previously unknown: "And I will make of you a fortress . . . ." From being timid, he has become a wall of bronze; from being a peace lover, he has become polemic and resistant; from being fearful, he has become capable of frightening others (they call him "all-round terror").

Thanks to his vocation, he acquires qualities he never thought he possessed. He experiences the calling as a rebirth, a vital recharging, a revelation of his true being, an unheard of promise of fecundity. For this, after twenty-three years, he feels the need to remember the event, so as to go on despite the tiredness, the bitterness, the disappointments that in the meantime had weighed him down (in the famous passages of the "confessions," he will describe himself as crushed by his mission). He feels the need to recall the fact that God has called him—root of his existence—to overcome depression and sadness. As he writes chapter 1, it seems clear to him that he has not placed himself in difficulty, but that the Lord has brought him on this path.

3. As a last path for reflection, I will suggest the comparative route. Jeremiah is a model to many vocations; we can better

understand ourselves in our weaknesses and in our strength when we see ourselves reflected in his image as in a mirror.

In particular I want to recall that even Paul saw himself in the calling of Jeremiah. When he seeks to understand himself, he relies on the great prophet. For example, in Galatians 1:15 where, recalling his life, he not only refers to the Damascus event but also to a certainty analogous to that of Jeremiah: "But when God who had set me apart before I was born and called me through his grace . . . ." ("Before I formed you in the womb I knew you, and before you were born I consecrated you"—Jer 1:5).

Paul knows that his vocation happened on the way to Damascus; nevertheless, he rereads his own existence meditating on Jeremiah. In fact, he invites us all to contemplate Christian life and our vocation in the light of the prophet, especially in his Letter to the Romans: "For those whom he foreknew he also predestined to be conformed to the image of his Son, in order that he might be the firstborn within a large family. And those whom he predestined he also called; and those whom he called he also justified; and those whom he justified he also glorified" (Rom 8:29-30).

If God has called us to be an image of his Son, he will not be disloyal to this calling, as he showed himself faithful in the life of Jeremiah, of Paul, and in relationships to God, who is the prototype of all vocations in Christ Jesus.

Contemplatio

At this point, let us shift from reflection to prayer, to the memory pleasing to God.

—How has the Lord called me to faith—through family, encounters, people who have helped me and have been close to me?

—How can my vocation to faith and to priestly, religious, or missionary life be the strength of my existence?

We have experienced—and perhaps will again in the future—difficult moments like Jeremiah, but we have the certainty that God has never abandoned us, that God is loyal to himself. Is such certainty profound and determining?

And, in adoring and silent contemplation, the Lord will come toward us with his grace as if it were the first day, allowing us to experience the joy of our original vocation, of perseverance in trials even marked by moments of discouragement and crises, the joy of loyalty to the mission entrusted to us, a mission that is personal and unrepeatable. The Lord will consolidate us on the rock of his love, and he will help us to believe that he is preparing great things for us that we must not fear; he will continue to operate forcefully within us and to enlarge our hearts to the horizons of God and of all humanity.

6.

The Man of the Word

We have seen who Jeremiah is, beginning with his calling, but I find it useful to try to define him with a characteristic that already emerged in his vocation but that expresses itself in his whole existence: He is the man of the word, the man whose destiny is somehow identified with the word of God.

At first, as a *lectio*, we will go through some texts that show the nature of the prophet's relationship to the word. In a second phase, in the *meditatio*, we will try to answer a fundamental question: What is my relationship with the word? Because the word, along with the Eucharist, is an essential reference point for the priest and, more generally, for each Christian.

Jeremiah and the Word

If we ask Jeremiah "How have you lived the word?," he will once again answer with images.

1. The Word as Fire. We find this image in a text of the so-called "Confessions": "Then within me there is something like a burning fire shut up in my bones; I am weary with holding it in, and I cannot" (Jer 20:9b).

For him the word was a fire that burned his bones, not a received concept stored in the mind; thus the force of his preaching is explained.

In another passage the same image is used by the Lord: "Is not my word like fire, says the LORD?" (23:29).

God himself compares his word to a fire that spares no one, does not leave alone, that consumes everything it touches. We should not limit ourselves to seeing it from afar, to admiring and hearing it. Nor can we take it in our hands without it changing us; one cannot let oneself be touched by fire and still remain unharmed, because if it gets to my hand, I am burned. Any contact with the living word enflames and agitates us, tends to radiate everywhere. In order to preach, theology is not enough; what is needed is the burning experience of our encounter with God. Religious concepts are not enough, and we must also be penetrated by fire.

Again, we read a promise by Jeremiah: "I am now making my words in your mouth a fire, and this people wood, and the fire shall devour them" (Jer 5:14).

The word that Jeremiah pronounces is a fire that first burns him and then others, all the while transforming them. Jeremiah therefore lives the word of God as an element that leaves nothing unchanged.

2. The Word as Unrest. What do I mean by "unrest"? To be precise, one would have to translate this second comparison with an inelegant expression: The word is like a "stomach ache," like a disturbance that gives no peace, no tranquility, that shakes up internally.

In fact, the prophet exclaims: "My anguish, my anguish! I writhe in pain! Oh, the walls of my heart! My heart is beating wildly, I cannot keep silent" (v. 19).

3. The Word as Hammer. Here is a beautiful image, the one of the word as a hammer that cracks the rock, as a heavy sledge. We find it in the verse of chapter 23 that we quoted earlier: "Is not my word like fire, says the LORD, and like a hammer that breaks a rock in pieces?" (v. 29).

4. The word as inebriating wine is another of Jeremiah's experiences. The word inebriates:

> My heart is crushed within me,
>   all my bones shake;
> I have become like a drunkard,
>   like one overcome by wine,
> because of the Lord
>   and because of his holy words (23:9).

These are all metaphors that indicate what the word means for us. It illuminates, informs, nourishes, and changes us, and at a certain point it opens us to new horizons, it stimulates us, moves us, has us falling in love or going out of our minds, out of the reasonability with which I calculate (I can do so much, I must do so much, etc.). The word pushes us to risk all for the love of Him who has spoken, challenging the unknown and the darkness. Jeremiah expresses himself with various images because he has really lived the extraordinary experience of this word and has been transformed by it. He even speaks of his resistance to the word that used to shake him, the word that he would have wanted to contain, but in vain.

5. Besides the four metaphors that underline the strong and explosive aspect of the word, I have chosen four others by which we can understand how the word is also a support for the prophet, a wall, a security, a comfort.

The interior dialogue that he lives with the Lord is the only strength on which he counts.

Such certainty was given to Jeremiah from the very beginning of his mission in the famous chapter 1:

> Do not be afraid of them,
> for I am with you to deliver you . . .

> They will fight against you; but they shall not prevail against you, for I am with you, says the Lord, to deliver you (vv. 8, 19).

And again:

> And I will make you to this people
>   a fortified wall of bronze;

they will fight against you,
>but they shall not prevail over you,
for I am with you
>to save you and deliver you,
>>says the LORD (Jer 15:20).

There are two significant passages in which Jeremiah himself underlines his total trust in the word:

O LORD, my strength and my stronghold,
>my refuge in the day of trouble,
to you shall the nations come
>from the ends of the earth . . . (16:19)

But the LORD is with me like a dread warrior;
>therefore my persecutors will stumble,
>and they will not prevail.
They will be greatly shamed,
>for they will not succeed.
Their eternal dishonor will never be forgotten (20:11).

There is a great affinity between Jeremiah's spirit and that of the psalmists, especially if we think of the psalms of trust and those of lament. The Psalter does not list the prophet among the authors of the psalms; however, without a doubt we find deep resemblances in the prayers and in the invocations to the Lord.

Therefore, on the one hand, God points out to his messenger situations of confrontation and difficult encounters, yet he assures him, nonetheless, that he will never be alone, that he has nothing to fear; on the other hand, Jeremiah experiences being able to always lean on God and in any case, with absolute certainty.

Meditatio: I and the Word

Reflecting on the texts and images that we have recalled, we feel a question springing up spontaneously: What is my relationship to the word?

For the sake of an orderly procedure, I would like to recall four moments in which the word, and especially the *lectio divina*, begins to relate to my life and my experiences:

—with effort
—with memory
—with affections
—with deep trust, which is the root of human existence.

1. *Lectio* and Effort. Daily effort is not caused by having to face certain difficult circumstances one by one, but rather by holding on, persevering to the end. It is a very difficult battle. All of us, in fact, are able to perform some strong act, one or two heroic choices, one or two important decisions; yet true effort is found in perseverance, enduring on the breach; it is a lifetime loyalty to God, to the ministry, to the Church, to the Eucharist, and to prayer. We do not say by chance that the greatest grace we can obtain is ultimate perseverance.

If this is then the basic struggle, as it truly is, then the most insidious temptation that corrodes our endurance internally is laziness toward life; it is sloth, tedium, banality, boredom, the tiredness of always being on the alert, of keeping watch. Jesus admonishes us: "Watch and pray so as not to fall into temptation" (Matt 26:41). The strongest temptation—even stronger perhaps than abandoning the faith or the priesthood—is to let it all go, to refuse to swim upstream, to give up the fight. There are persons who perhaps succeed in keeping up a certain exterior dignity, but internally they are burnt out, vanquished, resigned.

What relationship does the word of God, especially the *lectio divina*, have with the effort of perseverance, with the tiredness that comes from being vigilant?

—The *lectio* is first of all a continuous recharging of our motivation to endure, to not succumb, to keep hoping despite everything. It restores lost and worn out energies, it constantly stimulates our everyday routine. My personal experience is that when I am lacking contact with the word, I am deprived of that source of replenishment of the mind and heart that allows me to live, to always yearn for the better, to renew the guidelines of work for me and for others, to overcome moments of spiritual starvation, obscurity, impatience, disgust, and bitterness. The *lectio divina*, the word, is the gushing source that allows creativity and pliancy to pour forth. Jeremiah's "confessions" represent in a tangible way how a person can be tempted in perseverance while sustained by the word of God in this very temptation.

Furthermore, we must consider a more subtle relationship, namely, that of the *lectio divina* with the effort of vigilance.

Even though we are in touch with the infinite richness of God's word that nourishes us, at a certain point of our spiritual path, the *lectio* can—almost suddenly—become heavy, opaque, mute, like the village fountain that dries up after having quenched our thirsts for so many years.

The most dramatic, but also most significant moment of spiritual life comes just at the moment when God's voice seems to be silent. The whole doctrine of St. John of the Cross and St. Teresa of Avila culminates in the question: What sense can we give to the loss of the pleasure for God and the word of God? This topic needs to be faced because, sooner or later, depending on the various moments on the path of faith and prayers, we will feel it pressing within us.

The answer given by masters of the spiritual life is twofold:

First, the word does not speak or remain silent because we have been negligent. We presumed we knew it, so we no longer made an effort to analyze it, to listen to it with love, to capture in it the newness of God. In this case, we must diligently resume the exercise of the *lectio divina*, overcome the laziness that inevitably brings us to an interior state of internal stagnation, of confusion. It is necessary to humbly renew our attitude in front of the Lord and his word.

Second, it is nevertheless possible that the silence of the word is due to a mysterious trial we are about to undertake. This arid and dark silence becomes a purifying fire, and the suffering of whoever experiences it is great, so much so that one is tempted to abandon everything, to pray no longer, to spend time in different ways. In reality, if we persevere in this obscurity and darkness, if we remain firm in the trial, the Lord leads us toward a new knowledge of him; he returns us to a mute infancy in front of the word, to allow us to participate in his mystery of love, which is even beyond the word itself; he guides us toward the high peaks of his intimacy in the Trinity, where images are replaced by the divine Silence.

Naturally, we must ask ourselves: does the *lectio divina* no longer give me satisfaction because of my negligence or because the Lord is trying me? The answer is simple: if, despite the confusion and the total incomprehension of the word, I still feel the ardent desire for God and of the realities of my faith; if I continue to live the spirit of sacrifice in daily life bearing my burden and that of my brothers; if I do not feel attracted by the pleasure of the world, if I am willing to give myself for love, it means then that the word is nourishing me in secret by transforming itself into a desert manna that, seemingly tasteless, nevertheless nourishes the people on their path.

What is important, therefore, is to verify whether we are on the move or at a standstill; in the first case, the moment of the word's obscurity is not a going back, but rather a quality leap forward.

God, who is the Lord of our life and of history, knows when he must nourish us with the brightness of his colors (the taste for the *lectio divina*, the joy of reading the word) or when he must instead nourish us with night's darkness. It is always God who reveals himself in the word and who is hidden behind it.

2. *Lectio* and Memory. What do I mean by "memory"?

Psalm 119, at the letter *zain*, has eight full verses with the verb *zachār, zickrà*, namely, memory. More specifically, we find the word "memory" three times (precisely because it starts with the letter *zain*).

"Remember your word to your servant in which you have made me hope" (vv. 49, 52, 55).

The word has two ties to memory: First, it makes God remember his covenant. Through the *lectio divina*, I continue to

remind the Lord that I am his precious belt, his glory, his treasure, and to remind him of what he has done for me. Second,
the word makes present to my memory the name of God.

With the word we enrich our memory, and I underline this
aspect because I find it particularly useful. Today people have
difficulty remembering. Events occur so rapidly that any one
of them can make us forget the previous one. And television,
with its barrage of images, enables us to cancel past experiences. It is our society that has short memory, that does not remember history. For us, for example, Vatican Council II, which
we lived through, still represents a great event, but for the
young it belongs to a very remote past, as remote as Vatican
Council I or the Council of Trent. We are not a generation that
lives its memory; rather we live through images. When we ask
persons how they feel, how they have passed a certain time,
we realize that they usually answer beginning with their most
recent impression; if it is positive, all is well, but if it is negative, everything is going poorly, nothing can be salvaged.

Yet memory is actually the capacity of making a synthesis
of our lived experience, not to get stuck on a single experience
from which we judge everything. Memory is the remembrance
of the story that God has woven for us all through the days
and hence becomes a synthesis of gratitude and praise. This is
why the Bible is imbued with memory; "When I think of your
ordinances from of old, I take comfort, O LORD" (Ps 119:52).

And memory is fundamental for our most important life
choices. It is not unusual to meet people who are about to make
a wrong decision because, not remembering God's interven-
tion in their lives, they rely on feelings of discouragement, bewilderment, and solitude emerging from certain events as the
only key to self-interpretation. The true key to understanding
consists in the memory's endurance that allows us to objectively judge who we are, what we are living, and what we
have lived through the past twenty or thirty years.

What relationship does the *lectio divina* have with memory?

The word of God written in the Bible originates, in fact,
from the will of a people to establish a memory, not to trust in

the latest emotions or events, but rather to recall the marvels accomplished by God. The *lectio divina* puts us in touch with a culture rich in the memory of God's good deeds in the past, hence allowing me to go back to the good deeds done by God for me in my life, in the life of the Church, and of humanity.

The *lectio* is a continuous exercise of memory and, if many times we are able to overcome difficult moments, it is thanks to the memory of what the Lord has accomplished in me or in others. When, for example, I read of the sufferings of Jeremiah or of St. Paul, the memory of my own experience is enriched by theirs.

In conclusion, the *lectio divina*, the word of the Bible, is a school of synthesis of a lived experience that is personal, social, collective, ecclesiastical, and finally human.

3. *Lectio* and Feelings. Memory is not the only fundamental activity of humanity. There are also feelings, impressions, and emotions that come and go, escape us, or flow over us. Often we think we are making a decision based on logical reason, whereas we are dominated by a certain feeling or a strong dislike or liking. Sometimes, in fact, we realize that we don't have the feelings we would like. We would like them to be beautiful, orderly, profound, but instead we feel bereft of them. This means that feelings serve as our masters, so that a serious human problem is that of putting our feelings in order, of having the ability to keep our emotional state under control. This is the long educational path that we make children undergo on their way to reaching adulthood. Ordinarily, adults should in some way be able to control their affective world, but it is difficult, especially today.

The *lectio divina*, the word of God, educates us along the line of our feelings. Of course, we will never be able to fully control the realm of our emotions, feelings, and sensitivity. Yet this is perhaps good, since there is an element of surprise in the world of feelings.

Nevertheless, the *lectio* has a providential function because, if it becomes a daily habit, it results in a sort of reference guide for true and just feelings. I think of the orderly richness of the feelings and emotions of the psalms. I think of the stories of Abraham, Moses, of the Kings, of David, Jeremiah, of Jesus, and Paul, who all help us to distinguish in ourselves the negative feelings from the positive, the constructive ones from the destructive. When we read about negative feelings in Scripture, they become objectified, projected outside of us in a historical symbol or image, so that we can manage them more effectively.

How many times we have understood ourselves better by reading the stories of David or meditating on a letter of St. Paul, or a page of the Acts of the Apostles!

Actually, the psychological help received from psychoanalysis and its various therapeutic forms all have the same purpose; to objectify feelings in order to evaluate them and to be able to distinguish those negative, tumultuous feelings (that hurt, confuse, and bring to bitterness and nihilism) from the positive feelings that create trust, serenity, and perseverance in us.

But the Bible is an extraordinary school for the discernment of feelings because reflecting on my daily feelings and on those of biblical characters helps me to compare the emotive world of my passions and emotions with the clarity and order of God's mystery; I am invited to reflect on my feelings in and with Jesus.

The Bible lets me understand why I am sometimes sad and other times cheerful; why I go from enthusiasm to indifference or even to disgust.

There is a basic rule of evangelical feeling: to feel just as Jesus Christ

> . . . who, though he was in the form of God,
>   did not regard equality with God
>   as something to be exploited,
> but emptied himself,
>   taking the form of a slave . . .
>   and became obedient to the point of death—
>   even death on a cross (Phil 2:5-11).

The Bible, therefore, when known through the *lectio divina*, is an important and useful school that urges me to ask such personal questions as How do I manage my feelings? Do I fear them? In what order would I want them to be?

4. *Lectio* as a Gift and Letting Go. The three preceding reflections could make us believe that our relationship with the word of God is mostly active, that Sacred Scripture serves to overcome fatigue, to make a synthesis of our lives, to put order among our feelings.

Actually, the word of God contained in the Bible, before being an activity, is truly a gift of God. Through this word, God gives himself to me, speaks to me, nourishes me with his life, communicates his love, power, and divinity just as he communicates it to me in the Eucharist.

Therefore, my relationship with the *lectio divina* is an act of faith and trust in God, who reveals himself to me in Jesus, humble, poor, obedient, patient, and crucified for me. In this sense, it becomes a powerful antidote against a secularizing culture and civilization, against the culture of having, owning, building, and doing, where there is no place left for freely given gifts, where everything is calculated. When I practice the *lectio*, when I am in front of the word, I produce nothing, yet I receive a gift that marks me as a human being. I am human in so far as God gives himself to me in his Son and in his word. This is why I have on numerous occasions expressed my conviction, paradoxical as it may seem, that in our European world that is fast becoming more incredulous, atheist, and indifferent, a Christian is not able to live the faith without gaining familiarity with the word of God, through the *lectio divina*, without being nourished by such a word on a daily basis, and if each individual does not allow the mystery of divine grace to enter into his or her existence.

Prayer

After considering some images showing how Jeremiah lived his personal experience with the word, and having reflected on our personal relationship with this word, we are now called to the prayer that is praise and adoration before God, who wishes to encounter me in the silence of his mystery, well beyond any text or image. So, in order to enter into this unrelinquishable moment of the *lectio divina*, we can begin by saying:

> Lord, allow me truly to live with you and for you! Allow me to understand what Jesus, your living Word, is in my life, and how it sustains me in my daily trials. Help me to put my feelings in order, to dominate my emotions, and not to stop at first impressions. But most of all, let me experience the great gift you give me in your word.

7.

A Weak Voice

You, O Lord, through your Spirit, have not only inspired easy, consoling, and clear pages of Scripture, but also other pages that are heavy, difficult, obscure, and that make one feel ill at ease and embarrassed. We pray that you may clear all mist from our minds, so that we may seek what we are given to understand, and accept and revere what we do not understand, so that we can be prepared for that mystery of love in which everything will be unveiled, and we will know you as we are known by you, in your Son Jesus Christ our Lord.

Five Confessions of Jeremiah

Sacred Scripture presents us with some difficult pages that at times we are tempted to put aside. Yet if the Lord has inspired them, he certainly must have had a good reason, hence we are invited to investigate them.

Among these pages, there are certain passages of the "confessions" of Jeremiah, so called because the prophet speaks of himself, presents a kind of autobiography, and gives us to understand parts of what happens to him in the course of exercising his prophetic ministry. The title "A Weak Voice" refers to the group of five texts that I have chosen; Jeremiah—as we have already said—begins from the awareness of having heard a voice and of being himself only a voice. He does not perform miracles or heal; he does not raise the dead or have any power to punish those who do not listen to him; he does not threaten;

he has nothing but his voice. He is simply a man who speaks and nothing else.

The five confessions on which we dwell today are very well known yet, unfortunately, present a certain textual disorder. In other words, they have no orderly classification, but are like fragments put here and there so that it is difficult to understand if there is a progression among the various passages. Furthermore, if we consider them in their interiority, it seems desirable to arrange them with a minimum of logical development; Jeremiah appears confused in his thoughts; he goes from indignation to trust, then back to lamenting, reaching almost to despair. And the passages are difficult also for their content: everything seems negative, useless, to the point where a psychologist would see in these pages the signs of a depressive neurosis. Despite this, we must gain from these texts some specific teachings for our path.

It is certainly unexpected and unusual that a prophet in whom all of God's power resides, insists on describing himself as a weak person. Jeremiah is the word, his mission represents the word, but a weak one.

Perhaps his "confessions" attract and frighten us at the same time because we, too, experience ourselves as weak and, because the Church is weak, it has neither the economic power nor the ability to conquer the masses. Christians feel they are only a voice, especially in large secularized cities.

And there is more: Jeremiah is not able to show with extraordinary events that his word is true and, therefore he lives a form of pure faithfulness in regard to all that the Lord has him say. In the "confessions" we read both the weakness of the voice and how such weakness in no way affects the fidelity to the word.

Through these pages we will better know the figure of the prophet and also that of Jesus who wanted to be a humble and powerless voice; his weak voice is in fact a sign of his mission. We will understand something of the weakness of the Incarnate Word and that of a Church under constant persecution, whose offspring is sometimes tempted yet always faithful to its Lord.

Allow us Lord, thanks to Jeremiah's confessions, to delve into the mystery of your Son's incarnation, into the mystery of his unarmed condition, of his humiliation and of the poverty of our ministry. O Mary, mystery of humility and poverty, allow us to be transformed by the poor and humble life of Jesus.

The Meek Lamb (Jeremiah 11:18-23)

> It was the LORD who made it known to me,
>   and I knew;
>   then you showed me their evil deeds.
> But I was like a gentle lamb
>   led to the slaughter.
> And I did not know it was against me
>   that they devised schemes, saying,
> "Let us destroy the tree with its fruit,
>   let us cut him off from the land of the living,
>   so that his name will no longer be remembered!"
> But you, O LORD of hosts, who judge righteously,
>   who try the heart and the mind,
> let me see your retribution upon them,
>   for to you I have committed my cause.

Therefore thus says the LORD concerning the people of Anathoth, who seek your life, and say, "You shall not prophesy in the name of the LORD, or you will die by our hand"—therefore thus says the LORD of hosts: I am going to punish them; the young men shall die by the sword; their sons and their daughters shall die by famine; and not even a remnant shall be left of them. For I will bring disaster upon the people of Anathoth, the year of their punishment (Jer 11:18-23).

In this first confession, Jeremiah sees himself in a situation of persecution, in the image of the gentle lamb. The Lord himself showed him that he would be rejected and betrayed: "It was the LORD who made it known to me, and I knew; then you showed me their evil deeds" (v. 18).

We notice the surprise of a simple and naive man who painfully discovers that he is misunderstood by all his neighbors, his friends, and the people of his own land, Anathoth; he even discovers that they are plotting to harm him.

How can this be? The experts have some hypothesis. Probably in Anathoth, and especially in priestly families that had been excluded from serving in the temple, people were against the central focus of the temple as proposed by King Josiah; Jeremiah, on the other hand, was committed to a one and only temple, and all of a sudden he realized with alarm (from hushed phrases and strange gestures) that he was not well-liked and was actually the victim of suspicious plots.

We, too, experience bitter surprises when we discover that just where we thought we were supported and had found friendship, we've actually been misinterpreted; hence we suffer.

—Then rises in the prophet the great exclamation:

> But I was like the gentle lamb
>   led to the slaughter.
> And I did not know it was against me
>   that they devised schemes, saying,
> "Let us destroy the tree with its fruit,
>   let us cut him off from the land of the living,
>   so that his name will no longer be remembered!"(v. 19).

First of all, he seems to ask himself: But what have I said? I did not mean to hurt anyone! Then he relates the very harsh words pronounced against him that remind us of those whereby the Pharisees, right after Jesus' first miracles, decide to take his life. Through this confession we contemplate Jesus persecuted, who, from the very beginning, encounters the hostility of those whom he is helping.

Without a doubt there is envy in wanting to destroy the prophet at his peak, and outright hatred in wanting him to die: people were ashamed of Jeremiah and wanted to eliminate him lest the country no longer be sullied by his name.

—It is here that the prayer arises:

> But you, O LORD of hosts, who judge righteously,
>   who try the heart and the mind,

> let me see your retribution upon them,
>> for to you I have committed my cause (v. 20).

While the magnificent exclamation of trust in the Lord is understandable, because it expresses love, loyalty, and certainty in God who has sent the prophet, still we are embarrassed by the taste for vengeance that we see as another one of Jeremiah's weaknesses. But one must interpret his words of violence by reading them in the spirit of the psalmists, who put their cause in the hands of the Lord, leaving revenge up to him, knowing that only God is just.

In fact, verses 21-23 express the justice of Him who defends his prophet. Hence it is not Jeremiah who takes revenge.

Besides the surprise of not being supported by one's friends, I also wish to emphasize in the first confession the marvelous self-interpretation of the meek lamb that immediately reminds us of the pages of the canticle of the servant of Jehovah in Isaiah 53: "He was oppressed, and he was afflicted, yet he did not open his mouth; like a lamb that is led to the slaughter, and like a sheep that before its shearers is silent, so he did not open his mouth (v. 7).

We do not know if Jeremiah, with this image, wanted to refer to the prophet Isaiah, nor are we certain that the songs of the servant of Jehovah were already written. It is probably the author of these songs who received inspiration from Jeremiah by making a theological synthesis of his experience.

In any case, we have here two fundamental passages for the New Testament; the early Christian community, in an attempt to understand the mystery of Jesus' weakness and lack of defensive arms, found great enlightenment in the image of the gentle lamb. In this image it recognized the figure of the lamb of God sacrificed for our sins.

The Deceitful Brook (Jeremiah 15:10-21)

We see a second confession of Jeremiah after the passage of chapter 11, which in its great theological intuition allowed us to penetrate a bit more into the mystery of Jesus' humility and of his sacrifice.

> Woe is me, my mother, that you ever bore me, a man of strife and contention to the whole land! I have not lent, nor have I borrowed, yet all of them curse me. The LORD said: Surely I have intervened in your life for good, surely I have imposed enemies on you in a time of trouble and in a time of distress. Can iron and bronze break iron from the north?
>
> Your wealth and your treasures I will give as plunder, without price, for all your sins, throughout all your territory. I will make you serve your enemies in a land that you do not know, for in my anger a fire is kindled that shall burn forever.

> O Lord, you know;
> > remember me and visit me,
> > and bring down retribution for me on my persecutors.
> In your forbearance do not take me away;
> > know that on your account I suffer insult.
> Your words were found, and I ate them,
> > and your words became to me a joy
> > and the delight of my heart;
> for I am called by your name,
> > O LORD, God of Hosts.
> I did not sit in the company of merrymakers,
> > nor did I rejoice;
> under the weight of your hand I sat alone,
> > for you had filled me with indignation.
> Why is my pain unceasing,
> > my wound incurable,
> > refusing to be healed?
> Truly, you are to me like a deceitful brook,
> > like waters that fail.

> Therefore thus says the LORD:
> If you turn back, I will take you back,
> > and you shall stand before me.
> If you utter what is precious, and
> > not what is worthless,
> > you shall serve as my mouth.

It is they who will turn to you,
   not you who will turn to them.
And I will make you to this people
   a fortified wall of bronze;
they will fight against you,
   but they shall not prevail over you,
for I am with you, says the Lᴏʀᴅ.
I will deliver you out of the hand of the wicked,
   and redeem you from the grasp of the ruthless
      (Jer 15:10-21).

The expression "deceitful brook" is a very strong one that almost goes so far as to insult the Lord, to directly complain about him. It is a moment in Jeremiah's life that almost refers to a crisis in vocation. In my opinion, the expression "deceitful brook" expresses well the powerful experience of the prophet who feels tricked by his Lord, and even wonders if he has been abandoned. We can almost hear Jesus' cry on the cross: Why, O Lord, have you abandoned me?

The long passage begins with a lament that brings the mother into play: "Woe is me my mother, that you ever bore me." In these words there is all the pain of a person who feels completely alone.

And immediately comes the defense, the testimony of Jeremiah who fully knows he has obeyed the Lord, even if he now thinks that he is cursed: "Maybe Lord, I have not served you as best I could . . . ?" I have always been open toward others, I have done nothing to have enemies: Why has this persecution been waged against me?

From here comes the heartfelt question:

O Lᴏʀᴅ, you know;
   remember me and visit me,
   and bring down retribution for me on my persecutors.
In your forbearance do not take me away;
   know that on your account I suffer insult (v. 15).

In these heartfelt words the men of the New Testament will read and understand their persecution.

And, in verse 16, there is a splendid remembrance of the past. Perhaps it is the only time when the prophet admits that the words of God placed on his lips have not only been cause for suffering, but have also offered him moments of great joy:

> Your words were found, and I ate them,
>   and your words became to me a joy
>   and the delight of my heart;
> for I am called by your name,
>   O LORD, God of Hosts.

In happy times, Jeremiah loved and devoured the word that penetrated his heart. One recalls the story of the linen loincloth, where God said to the people: You are my name. "I did not sit in the company of merrymakers, nor did I rejoice; under the weight of your hand I sat alone, for you had filled me with indignation (v. 17).

Remember, Lord, that I have been so faithful as to accept to stay a distance away, to not even allow myself a private moment, to act always according to your word.

In verse 18b, the expression is harder: "Truly, you are to me a deceitful brook, like waters that fail." You are not a calm, reassuring river continuing to flow. We are at the height of temptation: Lord, now I know that you have abandoned me, you have left me without water, while I was counting on you, doing everything in front of you.

We must remember that Jeremiah may have lived for years in a state of muteness, unable to prophesy and to interpret what was happening among the people. It is a terrible suffering when a person who is no longer able to pronounce any words, after having had great courage to make a first announcement, remains gripped in a state of verbal aridity.

But just when he has almost arrived at a point of despair, his vocation is reconfirmed. "If you turn back I will take you back . . ." (v. 19). It is a difficult verse to translate, but one that shows very well the strong connection between the work of humankind and the work of God, the covenant understood as collaboration: If you do your part, I will do mine; if you come back to me, I will come back to you. Jeremiah knows that he cannot return to God if God himself does not call him, and the Lord reminds him of this by saying: Observe that we are one, that our work is one.

"And you shall stand before me. If you utter what is precious, and not what is worthless, you shall serve as my mouth." You will begin again to speak of me if, through this suffering, you will purify your desire to speak without first listening to me. We may assume that Jeremiah, in the aridity and bitterness of his trials, somewhat abandoned prayer and listening to the word. Then the Lord resumes the image of the earlier vocation: "I will make you to this people a fortified wall of bronze" (v. 20).

The prophet must have complete trust; whatever happens to him, he must believe in the promise.

If in the first confession there was a mention of an external persecution, in chapter 15 there is an experience of a more acute and intimate interior suffering because loyalty to God comes into question.

Why to Me? (Jeremiah 17:14-18)

The third confession is found in chapter 17:14-18, and we could name it: Why to me? Lord, do not assign me this fate!

It is, in fact, a heartfelt prayer that the persecuted prophet expresses against his persecutors:

> Heal me, O Lord, and I shall be healed;
>   save me, and I shall be saved;
>   for you are my praise.
> See how they say to me,
>   "Where is the word of the Lord?
>   Let it come!"
> But I have not run away from
>   being a shepherd in your service,
>   nor have I desired the fatal day.
> You know what came from my lips;

> it was before your face.
> Do not become a terror to me;
>> you are my refuge in the day of disaster;
> Let my persecutors be shamed,
>> but do not let me be shamed;
> let them be dismayed,
>> but do not let me be dismayed;
> bring on them the day of disaster;
>> destroy them with double destruction!

I emphasize just two things: The first is that of the persecutors who say: "Where is the word of the LORD? Let it come!" (v. 15). Here we read the temptation that Jesus suffered on the cross: if he is Son of God, let him come down from the cross and we will believe him! If what he has said is true, why doesn't the miracle occur? Jeremiah feels the people's mockery upon him: You are always speaking of the destruction of Jerusalem, of punishment, but why does it not happen? We want to see such things!

The second is the lament of the prophet for the incredulity, the lament that is expressed in a touching and somewhat naive way: "'I have not run away from being a shepherd in your service,' it is not I who wanted to pronounce such words, 'nor have I desired the fatal day, you know . . .'" (v. 16); "and therefore I beg you, 'do not become a terror for me . . . let my persecutors be shamed, destroy them with double destruction!'" (v. 18). Here we see again the desire for vengeance, which, as we have already stressed, is to be interpreted as Jeremiah's abandoning himself in the hands of God's justice.

A Very Great Suffering (Jeremiah 18:18-23)

Let us consider a fourth confession:

> Then they said, "Come, let us make plots against Jeremiah—for instruction shall not perish from the priest, nor counsel from the wise, nor the word from the prophet. Come, let us bring charges against him, and let us not heed any of his words."

Give heed to me, O LORD,
    and listen to what my adversaries say!
Is evil a recompense for good?
    Yet they have dug a pit for my life.
Remember how I stood before you
        to speak good for them,
        to turn away your wrath from them.
Therefore give their children
        over to famine;
        hurl them out to the power of the sword,
let their wives become childless and widowed.
        May their men meet death by pestilence,
        their youths be slain by the swords in battle.
May a cry be heard from their houses,
        when you bring the marauder
        suddenly upon them!
For they have dug a pit to catch me,
        and laid snares for my feet.
Yet you, O LORD, know
        all their plotting to kill me.
Do not forgive their iniquity,
        do not blot out their sin from your sight.
Let them be tripped up before you;
        deal with them while you are angry.

I will comment on the first two verses containing the essential part of this confession: "Come, let us make plots against Jeremiah—for instruction shall not perish from the priest, nor counsel from the wise, nor the word from the prophet . . . ."

What is the reason for Jeremiah's suffering in this passage? Not only because he is considered by his enemies neither priest nor wise man (which, however, he doesn't want to be) but because he is not even considered a prophet. In fact, they say: If we eliminate him, we certainly do not get rid of a priest or a sage or a prophet; he has none of these functions, therefore we must disregard everything he is saying. Jeremiah suffers immensely because he wants the word of God to be revered. It is the same suffering of the preacher or the pastor (be he priest or bishop) who realizes that he is not being taken seriously; people give no weight to his words, they listen but disregard it all and let it fall by the wayside.

The prophet, who lives only for the word and identifies with it, understands all the dramatic force of his enemies' opposition.

"O LORD, you have enticed me" (Jeremiah 20:7-18)

Surely, the most crude text, which we are considering last, is taken from chapter 20.

> O LORD, you have enticed me,
>   and I was enticed;
> you have overpowered me,
>   and you have prevailed.
> I have become a laughingstock all day long;
>   everyone mocks me.
> For whenever I speak, I must cry out,
>   I must shout, "Violence and destruction!"
> For the word of the LORD has become for me
>   a reproach and derision all day long.
> If I say, "I will not mention him,
>   or speak any more in his name,"
> then within me there is something like a burning fire
>   shut up in my bones;
> I am weary with holding it in,
>   and I cannot.
> For I hear many whispering:
>   "Terror is all around!
> Denounce him! Let us denounce him!"
>   All my close friends
>   are watching for me to stumble.
> "Perhaps he can be enticed,
>   and we can prevail against him,
>   and take our revenge on him."
> But the LORD is with me like a dread warrior;
>   therefore my persecutors will stumble,
>   and they will not prevail.
> They will be greatly shamed,

for they will not succeed.
Their eternal dishonor
   will never be forgotten.
O LORD of hosts, you test the righteous,
   you see the heart and the mind;
let me see your retribution upon them,
   for to you I have committed my cause.
Sing to the LORD;
   praise the LORD!
For he has delivered the life of the needy
   from the hands of evildoers.

Cursed be the day
   on which I was born!
The day when my mother bore me,
   let it not be blessed!
Cursed be the man
   who brought the news to my father, saying,
"A child is born to you, a son,"
   making him very glad.
Let that man be like the cities
   that the LORD overthrew without pity;
let him hear a cry in the morning
   and an alarm at noon,
because he did not kill me in the womb;
   so my mother would have been my grave,
   and her womb forever great.
Why did I come forth from the womb
   to see toil and sorrow,
   and spend my days in shame? (vv. 7-18).

As I indicated in the beginning of the meditations, it is impossible to know if this confession is really the last one in
chronological order. We are surely faced with a passage that
both frightens and attracts, since it expresses the bewilderment
of whoever has understood that while the Lord also has a very
heavy hand, nevertheless one cannot lack utmost trust in him.

"O Lord, you have enticed me, and I was enticed; you have
overpowered me, and you have prevailed" (v. 7).

God behaved with Jeremiah like a man who betrays a woman by first attracting her, then becoming her master and possessing her: you have seduced me, brought force against me, taken dominion over me and now I accuse you. I did not want to prophesy, and you have deceived me by making me believe one thing for another; you forced me to follow you without telling me what was coming; I had trust in you but you put me in extreme difficulty.

At times we, too, find ourselves in very painful situations in which we entered through obedience to God's law, to the Church, and to our vocation. But then surges in us a sense of rebuke and accusation: Why, Lord, what have I done to be so mistreated? I had faith in your word and in your promise, but I never thought that I would find myself without a way out, without liberation!

The consequences of this betrayal are dramatic.

> "I have become a laughingstock all day long; everyone mocks me. For whenever I speak, I must cry out, I must shout: violence and destruction! . . . I will not mention him, or speak any more in his name."

I am sorry I followed him, I no longer wish to listen to him, I can no longer endure. We must, however, observe that the lament is expressed in prayer, therefore with a spirit of faith, as Job would speak or as we read in certain psalms. We perhaps would not have the courage to repeat Jeremiah's outburst; we are in fact surprised that the Bible would relate it, since it almost seems a blasphemy: I will no longer follow you, I have decided to forget you. But if we reflect carefully on the text, we realize that these are words of love, of a passionate and irritated love, precisely because the prophet is not able to forget the One he loves. In fact, he continues thus: "Within me there is something like a burning fire shut up in my bones. I am weary with holding it in and I cannot" (vv. 7b-8).

This maximum expression of the strength of the word in Jeremiah is truly marvelous.

Verses 11 and 13 apparently lead to a solution of the conflict: "But the Lord is with me like a dread warrior . . . . Sing to the Lord; praise the Lord! For he has delivered the life of the needy from the hands of evildoers."

Here is another case in which the composition of the passage leaves something to be desired, since in the following verse the drama returns in even more inflamed tones. "Cursed be the day on which I was born! The day when my mother bore me, let it not be blessed! Cursed be the man who brought the news to my father, saying, 'A child is born to you, a son'" (vv. 14-15). And again in verse 18: "Why did I come forth from the womb to see toil and sorrow, and spend my days in shame?"

The lamentation closes tragically, and so the exegetes would like to change the order of the text placing verses 11-13 in the place of verse 18, so as to end with song and praise. Nevertheless, we must preserve the order sent down to us by Sacred Scripture, and we must therefore continue to question ourselves.

The Bible, in fact, is not only a pleasant spiritual nourishment, but it wants to shake us, upset us, and push us to wrestle with its pages for our own purification. Our quarrel with the word touches us intimately, and continuously invites us to rethink the mystery of God and to go more in depth, beyond those forms of religious superficiality that at times seem to satisfy us.

Meditatio: The Weakness of the Word

In the moment of the *meditatio* I think it would be useful to reflect on the weakness of the word of God.

We are servants of the word, upon it we have played out our life, we have committed ourselves to serve the Lord on his word and to place our trust in him. And suddenly we realize that the word is weak, it is not certain of success, it can be questioned, and does not have the power to perform miracles or to change situations. The faithful listen to us in part, but they mock and criticize us and do not give consideration to our preaching, which leaves us disappointed and perhaps frustrated.

1. Jeremiah's confessions bring us back to the weakness of the Incarnate Word, to the weakness of Bethlehem and Golgotha. Recalling this never convinces us fully, and there is always a temptation ready to emerge and provoke us: Why doesn't the Lord destroy the enemies, why does he not give to his Church strength, glory, economic possibilities, and the capacity to be successful in the mass media? Why must we battle every sort of difficulty? Jesus answers: Because in this way, I have revealed the Father. Especially in a course of spiritual exercises, we must place this mystery at the core of what the Lord wants to tell us; he recalls us to the humility of his word and of our ministry. It is a poor ministry, which cannot be compared to any human force, by virtue of which it is marked by a divine seal.

Let us recall, for instance, a page of Matthew's gospel where this fundamental truth is affirmed. He quotes a song of the servant Jehovah, wanting to make a synthesis of Jesus' suffering and preaching: "Here is my servant, whom I have chosen, my beloved, with whom my soul is well pleased. I will put my Spirit upon him, and he will proclaim justice to the Gentiles" (Matt 12:18).

The real preacher is neither a military nor an economic leader: "He will not wrangle or cry aloud, nor will anyone hear his voice in the streets" (Matt 12:19). A voice that is weak, just like Jeremiah's: "He will not break a bruised reed or quench a smoldering wick until he brings justice to victory. And in his name the Gentiles will hope" (Matt 12:20-21).

The hope of the nations is a weak leader, born in Bethlehem, who lived in poverty, was persecuted, imprisoned, tortured, crucified, and killed.

And Matthew comments on the ministry of Jesus with another prophetic word of Isaiah: "He took our infirmities and bore our diseases" (Matt 8:17).

Isaiah's intuition (as we already mentioned) probably came from reflections on the historic figure of Jeremiah, who took on the sicknesses and sufferings of his people, finally paying with his own life.

2. The mission of the Church consists in taking on the pain of the faithful in order to heal and relieve it, to help the poor and the hungry; but as we do this, we also take on our own weakness and poverty.

This weakness of the Church is best expressed in the most impoverished and defenseless reality that exists: the Eucharist. There is nothing more weak, more incapable of action, more passive than the bread and wine of the Eucharist; nonetheless, in it God fulfills the greatest revelation of his love.

Perhaps a lifetime will not suffice to fully understand this lesson; we tend to attribute a certain prestige and worldly power to our ministry and to the Church. Surely the Lord will grant us certain worldly satisfactions, but we need to know that the Church is more fully itself just when it is more similar to Christ of Bethlehem, to Christ on the cross, to Christ of the Eucharist, namely more like the weak and loyal voice of Jeremiah.

3. From the confessions, we glean one last teaching: even when the word fails us, when it is weak in us and we are gripped by discouragement and sadness, we are always servants of the Lord, and the sufferings we experience make us more like the gentle lamb. Therefore, to feel tiredness, disgust, discomfort, repugnance, or weakness is not at all contrary to our vocation; if we open our eyes, we realize that it is in these very circumstances that the Lord is truly present.

> Allow us, Father, to understand the mystery of salvation in the meek and defenseless condition of your Son, Jesus.

HOMILY

Wednesday of the Eighteenth Week in Ordinary Time, Cycle I

The Power of Intercession of the Church

The Figure of the Woman of Cana

Today the Church celebrates the memory of the holy Curé of Ars, who very much loved the Virgin, so I thought I would suggest to you a Marian reading of Matthew's text proclaimed in today's liturgy.

In order to deepen our knowledge of, and our relationship with, Mary of Nazareth, it is, in fact, important to reflect not only on the gospel passages that concern her directly but also on the episodes describing women similar to Mary and hence to the Church.

> Jesus left that place and went away to the district of Tyre and Sidon. Just then a Canaanite woman from that region came out and started shouting, "Have mercy on me, Lord, Son of David; my daughter is tormented by a demon." But he did not answer her at all. And his disciples came and urged him, saying, "Send her away, for she keeps shouting after us." He answered, "I was sent only to the lost sheep of the house of Israel." But she came and knelt before him, saying, "Lord, help me." He answered, "It is not fair to take the children's food and throw it to the dogs." She said, "Yes, Lord, yet even the dogs eat the crumbs that fall from their masters' table." Then Jesus answered her, "Woman, great is your faith! Let it be done for you as you wish." And her daughter was healed instantly (Matt 15:21-28).

Characteristics of Mary

Let us, therefore, try to capture in the Canaanite woman certain aspects that make her similar to Mary, Mother of Jesus.

1. She is, first of all, a mother who is not frightened by Jesus' refusal, and we recall a similar situation in the episode of the wedding at Cana. Jesus' mother tells him that the wine has run out, and Jesus replies, "Woman, what concern is that to you and to me?" Mary says to the servants "Do whatever he tells you" (John 2:4-5).

Mary, just like the woman of Cana, has unlimited trust in the power of intercession and expresses an extraordinary faith.

2. A second Marian characteristic of the woman of Cana is expressed in Jesus' praise: "Woman, great is your faith!" Elizabeth had said to Mary: ". . . and blessed is she who has believed" (Luke 1:45). Both are praised for their great faith.

3. The last words of Jesus to the woman who intercedes for her daughter are "Be it done unto you as you wish," and remind us, even if in a different way, of Mary's words to the angel: ". . . let it be with me as you have said" (Luke 1:38). We see the marvelous transposition: Mary asks for the fulfillment of the word that the angel had announced to her on the part of God; the Canaanite woman, who takes part in Mary's faith, deserves to hear such words said to her: May your word be accomplished. We can never reflect enough on this expression of Jesus who also represents, in a certain way, a reversal of the "Our Father," every time we pray "Thy will be done." Because Jesus, instead, turns thus to the woman: "Let it be done for you as you wish" ["Thy will be done"].

We enter more deeply into the mystery of the power of Mary's intercession, of the woman of Cana, and of that of the Church to which we entrust ourselves daily in the Eucharist.

Maternity

We know that the power of intercession is rooted in faith, namely, in God's mercy, but actually it is also rooted in maternity. The woman of Cana intercedes because she has invested everything in her daughter. She has put all of her hopes in her. Mary intercedes powerfully because we are her children. The Church uses all its power of intercession for each one of us.

Then another Marian and Church figure comes to mind: the widow of Nain (Luke 7:11-17) who, with her tears, intercedes for her dead son and obtains from Jesus the miracle of the resurrection.

Let us, therefore, entrust ourselves to the power of Mary's intercession, of the Church, and of the Curé of Ars.

> You, O Mary, figure of the Church and mother of all the saints, intercede to the Lord for our full forgiveness and the purification of the sins we have confessed; intercede for humanity sick and suffering, intercede for your people who love you so.

8.

The Solitude of the Prophet

The Prophet in a Deaf Society

Jeremiah is a very modern figure because he is the prophet of apostolic solitude, a prophet who speaks in a society that does not listen, just like our modern society. For this reason it seems important to me to understand more in depth the theme of the solitude of the priest or in general of the Christian, in an indifferent and secularized city.

I would like to take my inspiration for this meditation from an incredible and yet unheard word for the New Testament that sounds like a hammer blow: "The word of the LORD came to me: You shall not take a wife, nor shall you have sons or daughters in this place . . . ." (Jer 16:1-2).

It is not until we hear the affirmation of Mary of Nazareth, "I know not man," that we understand something of virginity or of celibacy for the kingdom. Jeremiah, therefore, is an exception in regard to the Old Testament, and in this respect his life is a prophecy. When attempting to answer the question "Who is Jeremiah?," we have said that he is a man who hears the calling, who relies completely on the word, he is the weak and humble man of the word. But he is also the man of a solitude marked precisely by the command of the Lord: do not marry, do not have sons or daughters in this place, as a sign. The prophet's existence matures in a type of solitude symbolizing the mystery of the presence of God in history that not only refers to celibacy but also to many aspects of his life (the prophet who was not heard, was mocked, and scorned).

First I will recall certain texts of Jeremiah, while later on I will consider a contemporary image that seems to me to correspond perfectly to the figure of the prophet. It is a French woman, Madeleine Delbrêl, who lived in the Paris suburbs and who had the extraordinary strength to be a solitary witness of God in the midst of militant communists. Personally, I esteem her as one of the great mystics of our century. Finally, we will ask ourselves what is the situation of the believer in the secular city.

As an introduction, I would like to offer an exegetical hypothesis for whoever would like to go more deeply into the topic.

This hypothesis tries to put order in chapters 11–20 of Jeremiah (containing the five confessions on which we have reflected), dividing them into two parts: the first from chapter 11 to chapter 15 (subdivided in its turn); a second one from chapter 16 to chapter 20 (again subdivided).

I will use a diagram:

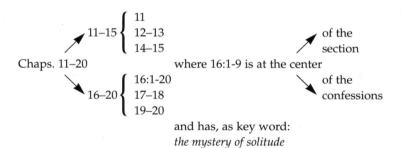

If we accept the two-part division, each ternary, it seems that chapter 16:1-9 (the prophet as solitary sign) is at the center of the whole section and of the confessions (the first two precede; the third, the fourth, and the fifth follow), whereby these frame the figure of Jeremiah as a solitary prophet.

I do not intend to go more in depth on such an exegetical hypothesis that, as with all hypotheses, has its probabilities and difficulties, but it is important for me to underline the Lord's word: "Do not marry, do not have sons or daughters in this place," because it is the key to all the ten chapters of the confessions.

Therefore it deserves great attention and we must ask the Lord to enlighten us:

> You who have given us a perturbing and new sign in the silence of your prophet in the midst of your people, allow us, as we penetrate into the mystery of Jeremiah's solitude, to participate in the mystery of solitude of your Son on the cross, and through it, reach out with love to all humanity. We ask this, Father, through Jesus Christ our Lord.

Jeremiah: A Man Alone

1. In Jeremiah 25:3, the prophet suffers the very difficult solitude of a person who is not heard. We have already considered the text, but we reread it with the new point of view.

> For twenty-three years, from the thirteenth year of King Josiah son of Amon of Judah, to this day, the word of the LORD has come to me, and I have spoken persistently to you, but you have not listened.

Jeremiah is not an isolated man; he always lives in the midst of people, he speaks, yet he is not understood, and for this reason he experiences a painful solitude.

2. In Jeremiah 20:8b, we read about the solitude of he who is mocked almost as if he were deluded:

> For the word of the LORD has become for me
> a reproach and derision all day long.

3. In Jeremiah 11:19 a third type of solitude, that of one persecuted, appears:

> But I was like a meek lamb led to the slaughter.
> And I did not know it was against me.

I was telling some of you about the testimonies of the bishops of Eastern Europe who have lived under communism: one spent twenty years in prison, another one became a chimney sweeper in order to hide, and still another (the current archbishop of Prague, Monsignor Miloslav Vlk) has for a long time cleaned store windows. They all would have wanted to announce the gospel but, at best, they had to do it in great secrecy because they were under constant police surveillance. This is somewhat similar to Jeremiah's solitude.

4. In Jeremiah 16:2 another painful form of solitude appears: the prophet does not even have a private life in which to take refuge: "You shall not take a wife, nor shall you have sons or daughters in this place." It is a new form of solitude, unknown in Israel.

But being deprived of familial affection is, however, a sign of the solitude of the people:

> For thus says the LORD concerning the sons and daughters who are born in this place, and concerning mothers who bear them and the fathers who beget them in this land: They shall die of deadly diseases. They shall not be lamented, nor shall they be buried (vv. 3-4).

Jeremiah is the symbol of the suffering and solitary people; he feels in his own flesh the people's drama, and, before curing the solitude of the people with oracles of consolation, he must first of all experience the suffering of many widows, of many young people, of many fathers, deprived of their most important affections.

His celibacy, although not for the kingdom in the New Testament sense, is nonetheless prophetic; in his own existence, Jeremiah summarizes poverty and the mourning of others, without having anyone to comfort him.

What message comes out of his solitude for the priest of today who, especially in the big cities is unheard or marginalized?

It is a question that beckons to us and that demands a clear and precise answer.

The Apostolic Solitude of Madeleine Delbrêl

The figure of Madeleine Delbrêl comes to our aid. Born in 1904, she embraces and experiences during her adolescence a lucid, reasoned, and decisive atheism; around the age of 20, she discovers God in such a profound way that he becomes Everything in her life, the Absolute. From that moment on (she dies in 1964 at age 60), she will be very faithful to the most radical essence of the gospel. And in order to devote herself to this God that represents Everything to her, she begins to search for the most suffering and marginalized human beings. In 1933 she joins some companions with whom she lives in poverty at Ivry, a completely secularized suburb of Paris. She herself will say: It is a people who has lost all Christian memory. At Ivry, in fact, Marxism reigns, and the Church means practically nothing; it is a very well-organized Marxism and very attentive to social problems. Madeleine, a social worker, wants to serve those in need, and to do so she is forced to begin mingling with the atheists around her. She will experience the terrible suffering of spending her whole life with the poorest for the love of God, without being able to share the fire of this love that consumes her: the people with whom she talks and collaborates feel her friendship, but they do not understand her mystery.

In such painful circumstances, she slowly elaborates an apostolic line of thinking and gives a provocative title to the only book she writes, *The Marxist City: A Missionary Land,* in which she presents her thesis.

It is a very simple thesis. Just when a secular civilization reaches the apex of denying God's existence, the Lord is present through the solitary force of a Christian witness. She writes this book for Christians, yet supposing it will perhaps be read also by Marxists, she says in the beginning that they will understand my wish to clearly distinguish their doctrine from my faith, and will understand that in so far as I love communists, I want them to take part in what for me is happiness itself.

Delbrêl also wrote some reflections and notes, and conducted many spiritual retreats for the small community she guided in the faith; all these words have fortunately been collected and we can, therefore, understand how she lived in the midst of the poor, always close to the sick, the unemployed, a form of continuous and extraordinary contemplation.

I have chosen a few of her thoughts on the solitude of the Christian because I see in Madeleine a Jeremiah of our times. Just as Jeremiah's solitude was a sign of God's presence, full of love for a people who did not listen to him, in the same way this woman conceives the believer's solitude in a secular society as not being a heavy, negative condition or condemnation, but rather as an occasion to proclaim the faith, to give witness to God's love for all.

What is, therefore, apostolic solitude?

1. First of all, solitude is "being with God." In this regard I will quote one of her poems, dated between 1945 and 1946, when she had already been living in Ivry for twelve or thirteen years:

> Our solitude, my God,
> is not being alone
> but Your presence, here.
> Because everything in front of You,
> either becomes death or becomes You
> (*What Joy to Believe!*—Gribaudi: 1969, 95).

It is a fundamental intuition: we seem alone, but actually the Lord's presence accompanies us with his love, and transforms us in him. She continues:

> To be alone
> is not to go beyond men or to leave them.
> To be alone is to know that You are great, my God,
> that You alone are great,

> and that there is no substantial difference between the
>   immensity
> of the grains of sand
> and the immensity of all human lives (ibid., 96).

It is not necessary to flee the world and human beings; on the contrary, we must be among them to serve them, since solitude is first of all a mystical perception of the infinity of God who fills everything with himself.

2. A second reflection: Solitude is the characteristic of missionary and apostolic life. I am reading some words that can sound exaggerated and that have to be understood in the context of the atheism in which Madeleine lived:

> The characteristic of a missionary community (namely, one that lives in an atheistic world) must be to form Christians not for a life of community, which is its normal attribute—this is the very Church—but to experience and live the faith alone, in a place where one is the only person to believe it.

She is concerned that a community of believers could become a small self-enclosed group, fearful of meeting the secularized and indifferent world. According to her, Christians of Europe must live community life in a parish or in a group in order to become able to live their faith alone where all others do not believe. In fact, in the last fifty years of urbanization, our experience has been that when people from the countryside come to large cities, they feel lost, lose religious traditions, and fall into indifference because they have not been educated to live a faith that can be expressed even in solitude.

But it is a solitude "not suffered with sadness, but rather accepted as the necessary condition for mankind having a vision of God." The Lord has sent me here to make me a witness to his word. For this solitude "must be faced directly from the very first encounter in an apostolic life, for all the cruel and necessary elements it contains for our very mission." For the person who loves the Lord, it is cruel to realize that in many hearts there is no correspondence with the love of God. And she relates one of her personal experiences (probably in 1956–57) when the worker-priest movement disbanded and many left the priesthood:

> During the last ten years, I have seen all too well how failures come about, hence I am struck by the important role played by solitude for which one has very little preparation.

In a dechristianized world it is difficult to persevere in faith if one has not been trained to live it alone.

> Those who have been victims of this solitude have borne it passively, allowing it to wear down their very psychological capacities; or they would rely on it as a moment of comfort, spending a few days in prayer alone, at least for as long as they had the strength to do so.

Whoever thinks it is possible to give witness to the gospel in a hostile world by withdrawing from time to time in a monastery or convent, thinking in such a way to preserve the faith, is in error; it is instead necessary to face the daily routine as an occasion to acquire strength, not to lose it. This intuition of Delbrêl seems to me extraordinarily new: to live one's faith in difficult situations is—as for Jeremiah—the victory of the power of the word.

> The solitude for which we Christians have not been prepared is the solitude of our condition as believers in the midst of crowds where our very faith placed in us an emotional desert. . . . We thought that for the apostolic Christian solitude was a kind of rare and precious luxury that allowed us to encounter Jesus more intimately and intensely. We didn't know that solitude would be an almost daily condition and that this solitude would be folly.

(The prose passages quoted above are from Delbrêl's *Community According to the Gospel*—Morcelliana: 1979, 101–102).

Solitude, therefore, is characteristic of missionary and apostolic life; if we see it as a painful and unpleasant trial, or rather as a personal intimate luxury, at a certain point we will lose our faith.

3. The third reflection is intended to ask a question: Why does Madeleine Delbrêl consider the experience of apostolic solitude so important?

It is because she understood that solitude ties us to humanity, allows us to understand people more closely, and puts us in touch with the most authentic form of suffering in Western culture, that of people who feel alone even if in the company of others.

I personally can tell you that I have acquired a very interesting perspective on the condition of youth today because so many young people write to me from all over Italy and abroad. The common denominator to all these letters from young men and women is fear, solitude, anxiety, even if they apparently are nonchalant, rowdy, and disco-goers. They feel alone in the midst of their activities and friends; they have no dialogue with their parents.

I believe this to be the secret of the suffering of the believer's solitude: by allowing ourselves to be fully immersed in it, we can understand and accompany our contemporaries.

Again, between 1956 and 1957, Madeleine writes:

> The knowledge of a human being almost always reveals (especially in large cities where people are uprooted and out of touch) a sort of inconsolable pain, a fatal form of solitude at the core of each individual's life that has a depressing effect until it is accepted as a personal choice . . . and is all the more acute as people are externally less alone (op. cit., 103).

Think of the solitude lived in the streets, in the buses, in the subways: everyone runs, is in a hurry, bumps into others without looking at them.

Now, in order to understand this anguish and remedy it, Jesus' task is to make us go through the experience of solitude, starting with the emotional solitude of celibacy. We are called to be consolers of so many of our brothers.

I can add that, today, the more people do not wish to experience solitude the more they actually do. If so many marriages fail, so many friendships and engagements are broken, it is because in fearing solitude, one pretends that the other fills his or her life, and therefore one takes advantage of the other instead of becoming freely more open. Any obsessive and possessive attachment is the death of communion between spouses and friends. Solitude, on the other hand, is the mother of communion. If I have learned to be alone willingly, I do not demand everything of others; I do not struggle to have others adjust to me, but rather present myself with simplicity, with my gifts, receiving with gratitude everything I get from others.

4. Here is another very meaningful thought of Delbrêl's:

> The person who seeks the love of God knows that this difficult solitude announces his presence. The person who seeks the love of human beings, the one according to God, knows that personal solitude has the power to achieve it, to accomplish true reunions with separations, misunderstandings, absences, because the unity achieved by love, just like everything springing from faith, is unshakeable.

We experience that God is God, that He alone fills our life, and we are able to announce it thus.

> If the solitude of the crowd comes to amount to this personal solitude, it means that God needs it (op. cit., 103).

God wants to make his presence felt through our experience in a desolate and anguished world.

It seems to me that in Christian communities such as parishes, oratories, and groups, the bemoaning of solitude, of being few, comes from the fact that we believe in our power—namely, if we were many we would be more powerful, we would be heard more—we don't believe as much in the power of God who manifests himself in Jeremiah's solitude.

Madeleine Delbrêl discovered that solitude itself (even if it comes from a negative condition) is the means by which the

Lord wants to save the secular city that is indifferent and steeped in a practical atheism that maybe speaks of God, but then lives as if God didn't exist.

The Lord creates a situation of solitude for the person having a serious, mature faith, for one who has carried out his or her life for the gospel, a condition that today is indispensable for apostolic efficacy.

The mystical intuition of this brave woman is profoundly similar to Jeremiah's intuition.

5. Finally, I will recall an annotation on prayer:

> Prayer cannot reach its greatest intensity without solitude. After Christ, even the saints had their deserts not always made of sand. In a crowd to which one feels connected, yet where one is solitary, we realize very acutely what "conversion" really means, the going back: it means going back completely alone, for oneself—because it is alone that one dies—and for everyone, in the name of everyone.

For example, we think objectively and realistically of the life of Teresa-of-the-Child-Jesus, of how she strongly felt the misunderstandings of her community, and to how she experienced solitude. Nevertheless, she did not dwell in resentment but rather followed the path of conversion, of her "little way," to live her faith perfectly also for others.

> One has to absolutely achieve a prayer of faith that abolishes relationships of force; I do not pray only when I feel strong, attracted by the desire for God, but I pray even when faith feels weak, because alone and not supported. The solitude of an atheistic crowd asks of us as a necessity that we return to a disrupted order, to a broken alliance, the recognition of a God who is the very purpose of our existence (op. cit., 105).

Precisely in this circumstance, prayer is a witness to God's greatness, adoration, intercession, and plea for all of humanity; it truly becomes prayer, that is to say, a force that changes life. We realize in this way that faith, foreign to the world, is a gift of God and is given as a gift to the world. We realize this especially when we have a relationship of friendship and walk along with a person of no faith. If we do not live such an experience, we run the risk of taking faith for granted, of thinking it is just a habit; it is mostly when we face such objections that we discover faith to be an extremely great gift of the Lord.

> Solitude represents the indispensable place for contact with God. Prayer strengthens its roots; our vision of any ecclesiastic community is transformed: Forests are made up of individual trees, each of which lives out of its own solitary roots. We learn that in order to offer us faith, God calls each one of us by name. We learn that faith is not a privilege we owe to heredity or our good conduct, but it is the grace of knowing that God gives the grace to be in the world dedicated with Christ to his work of redemption. . . . The solitude in which God has urged us to dwell makes us more aware of and in solidarity with each human being born into the world, with all the nations that God will summon on the last day (op. cit., 107).

For Madeleine Delbrêl, the perception of solitude (which is actually another way to say "the primacy of God") has become the essential condition to understand all, to love all, to feel humanity as one's own, to understand the poor, to offer one's life for the most abandoned human beings.

Nevertheless, we often think—because of the solitude of the secular city—that we are, so to speak, "the last of the Mohicans," the last to resist. This way of feeling is actually another way of expressing our meager faith, our incredulity. It is just in the moment when, through our grace, we recognize that God shows himself even in the secular city, that he has placed us in and for this society, that we recuperate the pride of our faith and the courage of giving witness.

The Believer in the Secularized Society

The believer in the secularized society, therefore, is the person who recognizes that the condition of solitude is not an obstacle; it would be one in itself, yet in God's power it becomes an exceptional springboard for faith. And in so much as we are priests, we must recognize that celibacy itself and the solitude in one's affections is the very place to understand people's suffering, to accept everyone's confidences, to be available to help others on their paths of quest. Celibacy, as a recognition of the primacy of the kingdom, becomes an instrument of communion. In fact, people have great faith in those individuals who live their celibate commitment with honesty and rectitude because they feel the value of this sign that Jeremiah was the first to establish.

To conclude, let us remember certain words of the gospel that strike me deeply because they translate with another language the experience of solitude:

> "Beware of practicing your piety before others in order to be seen by them; for then you have no reward from your Father in heaven.
>
> "So whenever you give alms, do not sound a trumpet before you, as the hypocrites do in the synagogues and in the streets, so that they may be praised by others. . . . But when you give alms, do not let your left hand know what your right hand is doing, so that your alms may be done in secret; and your Father who sees in secret will reward you.
>
> "And whenever you pray, do not be like the hypocrites; for they love to stand and pray in the synagogues and at the street corners, so that they may be seen by others. . . . But whenever you pray, go into your room and shut the door and pray to your Father who is in secret; and your Father who sees in secret will reward you."

And again:

> "And whenever you fast, do not look dismal, like the hypocrites, for they disfigure their faces so as to show others that they are fasting. . . . But when you fast, put oil on your head and wash your face, so that your fasting may be seen not by others but by your Father who is in secret; and your Father who sees in secret will reward you" (Matt 6:1-18).

It is interesting to note that these three indications all end with the same words. Know how to be alone, without witnesses in giving alms; know how to be alone, without witnesses, when you pray; know how to be alone, without witnesses, when you fast, because the Father sees your solitude and rewards you.

The clear and luminous relationship of each of us in solitude with the Father becomes the strength of salvation, that kind of strength that humanity needs so much, especially in the large cities tempted by secularism and indifference.

9.

The Passion of Jeremiah

Among all the prophets of the Old Testament, Jeremiah is undoubtedly the figure most similar to Jesus. We have already mentioned that Jesus' contemporaries recognized this resemblance; when they saw him in action they immediately thought of Jeremiah. We, therefore, ask the Lord to help us, through the meditations on the prophet, to better read the gospel and to understand more deeply the mystery of Christ.

Besides the characteristics and the aspects of Jeremiah's life considered up until now and that we find in Jesus, there is a passion, a *passio prophetae* very similar to Christ's passion.

It is amply described from chapters 36 to 40, and we will dwell on certain fundamental points to see just how this passion, this suffering, of the prophet speaks to us today.

I have divided the chapters, particularly dense, as a drama in five acts:

> —in the first act we take part in the drama of the book (Jer 30). It is interesting to see that first of all the passion of Jeremiah is that of his book;
> —in the second act, the passion of his person is narrated to us, with a first arrest (Jer 37);
> —in the third, the death sentence is narrated (Jer 38:1-13);
> —in the fourth act, there is a last dialogue (Jer 38:14-18) that recalls the one between Jesus and Pilate;
> —The final act is joyous because the prophet obtains liberation (Jer 40:2-4). The fifth act of the drama, therefore, shows a lack of similarity with the passion of Jesus.

1. The Drama of the Book

With the aim of grasping the dynamics of the whole story, let us first of all reflect on the passion of the book, which is the first to suffer; the fate of the prophet is already contained, preceded by the painful fate of the word.

> In the fourth year of King Jehoiakim son of Josiah of Judah, this word came to Jeremiah from the LORD: Take a scroll and write on it all the words that I have spoken to you against Israel and Judah and all the nations, from the day I spoke to you from the days of Josiah until today. . . .
>
> Then Jeremiah called Baruch son of Neriah, and Baruch wrote on a scroll at Jeremiah's dictation all the words of the LORD that he had spoken to him. And Jeremiah ordered Baruch, saying, "I am prevented from entering the house of the LORD; so you go yourself, and on a fast day in the hearing of the people in the LORD's house you shall read the words of the LORD from the scroll that you have written at my dictation (Jer 36:1-2, 4-6).

1. The narration is very incisive. It begins with the command given to Jeremiah to write; we are in 604 B.C.—"in the fourth year of Joachim." The prophet is 40-41 years of age, and although he has already spoken to the people, he has not yet begun to write anything, at least in an orderly form. Now, instead, his word becomes book; it is one of the moments in which the Bible is born, in which the spoken word becomes written—the order of the word is precise especially because the book will have a lasting effectiveness.

Jeremiah writes, as was common then, using a scribe, Baruch, who will take on the role of the prophet's secretary (we notice that it is the only prophet whose secretarial office is amply described). Why is it that he asks Baruch to take his place in the reading at the temple?

The reason is understandable: he already had a poor reputation and feared being seen in public. Although he had not yet been imprisoned, he probably felt he was under some surveillance. ("I am kept from going there and cannot go to the temple of the Lord").

The order to Baruch to read is very clear:

> . . . so you go yourself, and on a fast day in the hearing of the people in the LORD's house you shall read the words of the LORD. . . . You shall read them also in the hearing of the people of Judah who come up from their towns (v. 6).

2. The story then reports three readings.

The first reading is indicated in verse 8: "And Baruch son of Neriah did all that the prophet Jeremiah ordered him about reading from the scroll the words of the LORD in the LORD's house."

But the reading gives rise to scandal, great worry, attention, and surprise, so the leaders of the people who were not in the temple at that time, send to Baruch Jehudi, son of Nethaniah son of Shelemiah, the son of the Ethiopian inviting him to go to them. There is then a second reading: "So Baruch son of Neriah took the scroll in his hand and came to them. And they said to him, 'Sit down and read it to us.'" The book being read and reread makes one understand the advantage of the written word that can thus be repeated. "When they heard all the words, they turned to one another in alarm, and said to Baruch, 'We certainly must report all these words to the king'" (see vv. 9-16).

The third reading is done in front of the king by Jehudi, and this is the first passion. The passage is horrifying because it underlines atheism and the incredulity of King Joachim.

> Now the king was sitting in his winter apartment (it was the ninth month), and there was a fire burning in the brazier before him. As Jehudi read three or four columns, the king would cut them off with a penknife and throw them into the fire in the brazier . . . (vv. 22-23).

The word is, therefore, destroyed, burned, as if to say: it should absolutely not exist. The person who rejects the word of God not only refuses to hear it, but goes so far as not wanting it to exist. Jesus immediately comes to mind, living Word of the Father, put to death because he must no longer exist.

The Lord nevertheless intervenes and what follows death is the resurrection of the Word.

> Now, after the king had burned the scroll with the words that Baruch wrote at Jeremiah's dictation, the word of the LORD came to Jeremiah: Take another scroll and write on it all the former words that were in the first scroll . . . (vv. 27-28).

But in the meantime the word has experienced a very painful event.

2. The Drama of the Person: The First Arrest

In the episode of chapter 36 we have seen that Jeremiah had remained untouched and unharmed, while in chapter 37 his personal drama begins. Here it is a matter of a rather bland suffering, since he is imprisoned because of a misunderstanding, not through persecution. There is even a comical twist to this imprisonment—the prophet wants to leave Jerusalem to go to the land of Benjamin to receive his share of property among the people there, but one of the king's guards, thinking that he wanted to cross over to the enemy, then arrests him:

> "You are deserting to the Chaldeans." And Jeremiah said, "That is a lie; I am not deserting to the Chaldeans." But Irijah [the guard] would not listen to him and arrested Jeremiah and brought him to the officials. The officials were enraged at Jeremiah, and they beat him and imprisoned him in the house of the secretary Jonathan, for it had been made a prison. Thus Jeremiah was put in the cistern house, in the cells, and remained there many days (Jer 37:13-16).

We notice here the similarity between the imprisoned prophet and Jesus imprisoned who, during the night waits for hours in solitude for the first pronouncement, the first sentence.

Here the questioning is done personally by the king: "Then King Zedekiah sent for him, and received him. The king questioned him secretly in his house, and said: Is there any word

from the LORD?" (v. 17). The word is both splendid and terrible, but Jeremiah, although he is afraid of the prison, does
not conceal it, nor is he concerned with saying it somewhat
gracefully. In fact, he answers: "There is!," and more precisely:
"You shall be handed over to the king of Babylon." And after
having spoken so courageously to Zedekiah, he downright
complains about his unjust suffering: "What wrong have I
done to you or your servants or this people, that you have put
me in prison?" (v. 18).

Let us recall Jesus' question to the guard who is beating him:
"If I have spoken wrongly, testify to the wrong. But if I have
spoken rightly, why do you strike me?" (John 18:23). Jeremiah,
therefore, defends himself and, furthermore, not being a hero,
begs the king not to send him to the previous prison: "Now,
please hear me, my lord king: be good enough to listen to my
plea, and do not send me back to the house of the secretary
Jonathan to die there" (v. 20). It is moving to see prophet's humanity. He does not want to die and he asks the king to at least
put him in a better prison. Strangely, Zedekiah, who has listened to a very hard message, has pity on him and gives orders: ". . . and they committed Jeremiah to the court of the
guard; and a loaf of bread was given him daily from the bak-
ers' street, until all the bread of the city was gone. So Jeremiah
remained in the court of the guard" (v. 21).

In this way ends the second act of the drama regarding the
very person of the prophet; Jeremiah, everything considered,
is treated rather favorably.

3. The Death Sentence

We read in chapter 38:

> Now Shephatiah son of Mattan, Gedaliah son of Pashhur, Jucal
> son of Shelemiah, and Pashhur son of Malchiah heard the
> words that Jeremiah was saying to all the people, Thus says the
> LORD, Those who stay in this city shall die by the sword, by
> famine, and by pestilence; but those who go out to the Chal-

deans shall live; they shall have their lives as a prize of war, and live. Thus says the LORD, This city shall surely be handed over to the army of the king of Babylon and be taken. Then the officials said to the king, "This man ought to be put to death, because he is discouraging the soldiers who are left in this city, and all the people, by speaking such words to them. For this man is not seeking the welfare of this people, but their harm." King Zedekiah said, "Here he is; he is in your hands; for the king is powerless against you." So they took Jeremiah and threw him into the cistern of Malchiah, the king's son, which was in the court of the guard, letting Jeremiah down by ropes. Now there was no water in the cistern, but only mud, and Jeremiah sank in the mud.

Ebed-melech the Ethiopian, a eunuch in the king's house, heard that they had put Jeremiah into the cistern. The king happened to be sitting at the Benjamin Gate, So Ebed-melech left the king's house and spoke to the king, "My lord king, these men have acted wickedly in all they did to the prophet Jeremiah by throwing him into the cistern to die there of hunger, for there is no bread left in the city." Then the king commanded Ebed-melech the Ethiopian, "Take three men with you from here, and pull the prophet Jeremiah up from the cistern before he dies." So Ebed-melech took the men with him and went to the house of the king, to a wardrobe of the storehouse, and took from there old rags and worn-out clothes, which he let down to Jeremiah in the cistern by ropes. Then Ebed-melech the Ethiopian said to Jeremiah, "Just put the rags and clothes between your armpits and the ropes." Jeremiah did so. Then they drew Jeremiah up by the ropes and pulled him out of the cistern. And Jeremiah remained in the court of the guard (Jer 38:1-13).

Jeremiah faces a real danger of death that, thanks to the Ethiopian and King Zedekiah, changes into a hard prison sentence.

Verse 4 is especially interesting: "Then the officials said to the king, 'This man ought to be put to death, because he is discouraging the soldiers who are left in this city, and all the people, by speaking such words to them. For this man is not seeking the welfare of this people, but their harm.'" It is the same accusation brought against Jesus: He agitates the people, he does not think of the good of the people, the Romans will come against us—Jesus must die. There is, therefore, a real parallel with Jesus' passion.

Verse 7, which tells about Jeremiah sunk in the mud, helps us to better understand certain psalms, for instance Psalm 130: "Out of the depths I cry to you, O Lord," which we can interpret as the cry of Jeremiah from the bottom of the mud-filled well, "Lord, hear my voice."

Nevertheless, Jeremiah is protected, the Ethiopian intercedes, speaks to the king of his miserable condition, and Zedekiah has him freed and saves him, so to speak, at the last minute.

4. The Last Dialogue

The fourth act of the drama, the last of the *passio prophetae,* presents the dialogue with King Zedekiah, who has saved him:

> King Zedekiah sent for the prophet Jeremiah and received him at the third entrance of the temple of the LORD. The king said to Jeremiah [we notice the similarity with the questions posed to Jesus during his passion]: "I have something to ask you; do not hide anything from me" Jeremiah said to Zedekiah, "If I tell you, you will put me to death, will you not? And if I give you advice, you will not listen to me." So King Zedekiah swore an oath in secret to Jeremiah, "As the LORD lives, I will not put you to death or hand you over to these men who seek your life" (Jer 38:14-16).

I emphasize the fact that this dialogue has also penetrated the texts of the New Testament. In Luke 22:67, Jesus is interrogated by the grand council of the Sanhedrin: "'If you are the Messiah, tell us.' He replied, 'If I tell you, you will not believe; and if I question you, you will not answer.'" Some texts add the following: "'If I say it, it is certain that you will have me die, and if I give you advice, you will not listen to me.'" This means that the first Christian writers purposely put Jeremiah's answer on Jesus' lips.

Yet Zedekiah has a bigger heart than the men of the Sanhedrin, and he promises the prophet that he will not harm him.

> Then Jeremiah said to Zedekiah, "Thus says the LORD, the God of hosts, the God of Israel, If you will only surrender to the officials of the king of Babylon, then your life shall be spared, and this city shall not be burned with fire, and you and your house shall live. But if you do not surrender to the officials of the king of Babylon, then this city shall be handed over to the Chaldeans, and they shall burn it with fire, and you yourself shall not escape from their hand." King Zedekiah said to Jeremiah, "I am afraid of the Judeans who have deserted to the Chaldeans, for I might be handed over to them and they would abuse me." Jeremiah said, "That will not happen. Just obey the voice of the LORD in what I say to you, and it shall go well with you, and your life shall be spared. But if you are determined not to surrender, this is what the LORD has shown me—a vision of all the women remaining in the house of the king of Judah being led out to the officials of the king of Babylon . . ." (Jer 38:17-22).

It is the last dialogue of the prophet with the king, the last dialogue with his people, because here ends the passion of Jeremiah.

5. Liberation

In fact, he will be freed, but by the enemies of Israel, the Chaldeans; he will be freed by King Nebuchadrezzar's troops. When the troops will have captured all the prisoners and will have brought them to Ramah, the head of the guard, Nebuzaradan, will go to take Jeremiah, who was staying with the other prisoners and will say to him:

> The LORD your God threatened this place with this disaster; and now the LORD has brought it about, and has done as he said, because all of you sinned against the LORD and did not obey his voice. Therefore this thing has come upon you. Now look, I

have just released you today from the fetters on your hands. If you wish to come with me to Babylon, come, and I will take good care of you; but if you do not wish to come with me to Babylon, you need not come. See, the whole land is before you; go wherever you think it good and right to go (Jer 40:2-4).

Jeremiah will first experience the fate of those who suffer, in Jerusalem, and then that of the exiles in Egypt, where he will die in obscurity. His life ends without glory and, at a certain point, his voice simply fades away; after having completed the mission of announcing the Lord's presence in the punishment of the city, the prophet is silent and no longer speaks. We know that his character will never be forgotten and that his teaching of a new covenant and a religion of the heart will have an influence on the purest line of Judaism, preparing the new covenant of Jesus.

Reflections for the *Meditatio*

A spontaneous question arises: Why is the story of Jeremiah's passion so long? If it were to have a dramatic conclusion, if the prophet were to go from the announcement to prison, then to a sentence followed by torture and death, we would find such a lengthy description of martyrdom logical. But Jeremiah is not a martyr. He is simply a prophet who obeys the word.

What meaning then can we find in this story that bears so many similarities as well as differences with the passion of Jesus?

After reading and meditating on chapters 36–40, I seem to have grasped at least four meanings that justify it and provide as many messages for us.

1. Usually our sufferings cannot be compared to those of Jesus, except for martyrs who profess their faith by shedding their blood.

Our life is often less glorious because we go from suffering to liberation, from difficult and obscure moments to easier ones, from dramatic and sometimes heroic situations to more ordinary ones.

Certainly for all of us there is the finality of death to which we are called to give witness, yet it does not always seem to be the climax of an apostolic existence. We can anticipate death rather in small sufferings, where we need to know how to understand the final task that awaits us when we will be asked, as Jesus was, to abandon our life to the hands of God. Jeremiah, therefore, teaches us to experience the small, painful, and sometimes even great loyalties of our daily lives.

2. Jeremiah, who is not a martyr, is not even a hero; he is afraid of death. In fact, he begs the king to remove him from an awful prison and to allow him an easier, more livable one, and he is happy when he is freed.

Neither are we heroes, and we need to know and accept ourselves for what we are because the Lord sees our weakness, our fear of suffering, of persecution, and of martyrdom. There is a reason why the early Christians did not approve of a person of faith who would spontaneously go to the emperors, to the enemies of Christ to receive martyrdom; they considered such an initiative an act of pride and presumption.

If we face any sort of trial, we must accept it with the conviction that the Lord has sent it for our good; we must, therefore, accept our poverty, our not wanting to be immersed in suffering, and our rejecting the cross when we think that it does not correspond to God's mysterious ways. This is an invitation to have a great awareness of our own fragility and to humbly trust in the Lord.

3. However, in all his weakness, Jeremiah stands out for his unshakeable faith in God's word. He fears prison and death, but he knows how to announce and tell of God's word without a second of hesitation and, before the king, he clearly and explicitly says: You will fall into the hands of the enemy, you will be imprisoned, you must surrender.

The word is much stronger than he is and, despite everything, he is faithful to it. This is the grace we must ask for. Not to have an always heroic courage, but rather the grace to say, to do, to express each time what truly corresponds to our mission, to be faithful to our mandate, to fulfill daily acts of loyalty. Jeremiah's message is not resounding or glorious. It is humble, a simple message for daily living. And he warns us: Do not seek to be heroes, but be happy to live patiently the faithfulness of the word day after day; do not be frightened by your fears and shyness, because I, too, have experienced them.

4. One last reflection. The story of Jeremiah and his passion shows how Jesus' story is much more dramatic. There are some similarities between them, but Jesus pays his faithfulness to the Father with his life, not only with prison.

Our eyes then turn constantly to Him because he is the only one who fully inspires us; the prophets are great men of God, Jeremiah is one of the greatest, but Jesus is truly the only great one who inspires us.

We can conclude our meditation by gazing at the crucifix and meditating thus:

> Lord, you have truly suffered in terribly dramatic circumstances for your loyalty and witness to your message. You have come among us in order to be faithful to the mandate of the Father and to teach us to be faithful as well. In order to redeem us, you have shunned no pain, no insult, not a single moment of your passion; for our happiness, you have surrendered to death. Help us, we pray, to fully enter into the mystery of your faithfulness!

10.

The Prophet Who Consoles

Jeremiah's Point of Arrival

> O Lord, who have inspired Jeremiah with the words of consolation, place on our lips and in our hearts your gospel, so that we can bring comfort and joy to those who suffer in desolation and in obscurity. We ask you this, Father, through Christ our Lord.

After the meditation on the purification of the heart and while we ask ourselves just what is the will of God for us, for me, we want to approach the decisive pages of the prophet Jeremiah, the ones for which the book was written. Without them, in fact, they would be almost incomprehensible, full as they are of laments, threats, and punishment. These pages, in fact, give more meaning to the other passages and are even fundamental for our lives as priests, bishops, ministers of the New Testament, and servants of a new covenant.

In the chapters we will read, we will see that the formula of the new covenant is the mature fruit of the work realized by God in Jeremiah. We can say that the suffering, pains, trials, humiliations, and the passion of the prophet all find their fruition in the expression "the new covenant." Therefore, in this meditation, we somehow gather the fruits of the path we have followed in these exercises (the burden, the prayer, the contemplation) to then apply them to our ministry.

The "consoling prophet" is truly the end-point of everything we have tried to say on the figure of Jeremiah; he has become the man of the word, he has suffered the weakness of the word, he has passed through purification and temptation because he needed to become a prophet able to console, to give joy, to comfort. It is especially in chapters 30–33 that he becomes an evangelist, the announcer of the good news of that new covenant on which our lives are based and to which we have dedicated our whole being. We will dwell on certain passages, on a few decisive texts of those chapters, focusing most of all on a gesture, on a symbol, because Jeremiah speaks mainly through symbols; later, in a second phase, we will consider the oracles; then we will ask ourselves how the oracle of consolation originates and where the power to console comes from. In this way we will find help to reflect on ourselves, to understand how the power to announce the gospel of consolation is born in us, and finally to know if we are truly capable of consoling our people.

1. The Gesture of Consolation

Chapter 32 is long and very beautiful; I invite you to read it carefully and slowly, appreciating it word for word, because it is a synthesis of all Jeremiah's prophecy and explains its aim to us. I will only underline the parts that are more specifically symbolic.

—The gesture of consolation occurs in the third act of the drama on which we have reflected in the preceding meditation, namely, from the moment Jeremiah is imprisoned to the time of King Zedekiah; a rather mild form of prison that nevertheless is already a form of persecution. "The word that came to Jeremiah from the Lord in the tenth year of King Zedekiah of Judah, which was the eighteenth year of Nebuchadrezzar. At that time the army of the king of Babylon was besieging Jerusalem, and the prophet Jeremiah was confined . . . in the palace of the king of Judah . . ." (Jer 32:1-2).

—While in prison, Jeremiah hears a very precise word of the Lord: "Hanamel son of your uncle Shallum is going to come to you and say, 'Buy my field that is at Anathoth, for the right of redemption by purchase is yours'" (v. 7). An apparently absurd word, since the enemies occupied even that camp, and the city was about to be destroyed. Nevertheless, Jeremiah listens to the Lord and, when the family member comes asking to buy the field, he acts in a way that is accurately described:

> And I bought the field from Anathoth from my cousin Hanamel, and weighed out the money to him, seventeen shekels of silver. I signed the deed, sealed it, got witnesses and weighed the money on scales. Then I took the sealed deed of purchase, containing the terms and conditions, and the open copy; and I gave the deed of purchase to Baruch son of Neriah son of Mahseiah, in the presence of the witnesses who signed the deed of purchase, and in the presence of all the Judeans who were sitting in the court of the guard (vv. 9-12).

The symbolic gesture is enigmatic, but we read its meaning immediately following:

> In their presence I charged Baruch, saying, Thus says the LORD of hosts, the God of Israel: Take these deeds, both this sealed deed of purchase and this open deed, and put them in an earthenware jar, in order that they may last for a long time. For thus says the LORD of hosts, the God of Israel: Houses and fields and vineyards shall again be bought in this land (vv. 13-15).

It is very interesting to observe the custom of preserving important documents in earthen vases, jars, or clay pots; thanks to this custom, after two thousand years, we've been able to find the manuscripts of Qumram well-sealed in clay pots.

—Now we understand Jeremiah's gesture: he accomplishes a prophetic act whose realization he will not see because it is projected for the future: "Yes, they will still buy homes, fields and vineyards," since that land, destined for destruction, will return to life.

It is the last symbol through which the prophet expressed himself, and that serves as a stabilizing force for all the rest— the rotten loincloth, the broken jug, the potter, the wine-jar— disconcerting objects for the sadness and misfortune to which they alluded. The act of the purchase of the field is full of hope, true hope, inviting people to throw an anchor toward the future and to look at God's future. It has, therefore, a deeply consoling effect, almost as if to say: no, not all is lost. It expresses in a symbol the whole substance of the chapters on consolation.

2. Words of Consolation

We mostly read about the long oracles that amplify the meaning of the symbolic act in chapters 30–31.

I will dwell especially on Jeremiah 31:31-34, verses we know well because in them the Old Testament reaches its highest pinnacle and speaks fully to us. The New Testament understood quite well that here it is a matter of crucially important words, making this clear by relating them in their original entirety. The first Christians actually learned them by heart, and through them they understood themselves; these words are related in their entirety in the Letter to the Hebrews, chapter 8, verses 8-12 (the longest quote made in the New Testament of a passage of the Old Testament). We repeat them daily in the Eucharist because they mark the Eucharistic institution as a sign of the new covenant.

> The days are surely coming, says the LORD, when I will make a new covenant with the house of Israel and the house of Judah. It will not be like the covenant that I made with their ancestors when I took them by the hand to bring them out of the land of Egypt—a covenant that they broke, though I was their husband, says the LORD. But this is the covenant that I will make with the house of Israel after those days, says the LORD: I will put my law within them, and I will write it on their hearts; and I will be their God, and they shall be my people. No longer shall they teach one another, or say to each other, "Know the LORD," for they shall all know me, from the least of them to the greatest, says the LORD, for I will forgive their iniquity, and remember their sin no more (Jer 31:31-34).

There are, therefore, four characteristics of the new covenant. The Lord will place his law in our heart; then he will truly be our God and we will truly be his people; we will no longer have to mutually teach each other because we will all know the Lord; he will forgive our iniquities and will no longer remember our sins.

On the one hand, this covenant is the same as that of Sinai, expressed with an identical formula ("I will be their God, and they shall be my people") that we will find again along the path of the Old Testament, even if in different terms: the covenant is characterized by mutual adherence, mutual belonging. John, the evangelist, often repeats the formula of the covenant with words to this effect: "Abide in me as I abide in you" (John 15:7), and again: ". . . abide in my love" (John 15:9).

On the other hand, in reference to the pact of Sinai, Jeremiah underlines the interiority ("I will put my law within them, and I will write it in their hearts"). Therefore, while in the Old Testament, the law was transmitted from father to son, in the New Testament the law is the Holy Spirit, according to the well-known expression of Thomas Aquinas: *Nova lex principaliter in Spiritu sancto consistit.* Jeremiah, therefore, preannounces a knowledge of God no longer through the mediation of the Law but through an interior awareness in which the Law enters the heart. In no way does this make either the observation of the law or its external expression useless, but it simply appears to be secondary; what is primary is each human being's personal relationship with God.

We are faced here with a very profound intuition of the prophet that emerges as a spiritual climax to all the other oracles of his book. And this new covenant also includes a definite forgiveness. It is a promise of that mercy and grace that will flow from the pierced heart of the crucified Christ. Jesus, who on the cross forgives and spreads the Spirit, is the clear sign of the new covenant rooted in Sinai; the new covenant is Christ, who gives his body and blood in the Eucharist for the remission of all sins.

Jeremiah 31:31-34 is the most important passage in the entire Old Testament.

3. The Origin of Consolation

Is it possible to describe the pedagogical itinerary through which God led his prophet to such a revelation?

Scholars are convinced that there is such an itinerary, that the perception of consolation does not come to Jeremiah suddenly from heaven, but rather it was formed in him, thanks to a long and arduous path that I wish to recall here briefly.

The genesis of chapters 30 to 31 can be divided into three important moments: the time of joy, the time of defeat, and the time of broadened horizons.

a) Initially they emerge in a time of particular euphoria, joy, enthusiasm, and trust; it is the golden moment immediately following Josiah's reform in the year 622 b.c. Jeremiah has had his first vocation and is becoming an adult, his age is between twenty-three and twenty-five (assuming he was born in 645). The king has accomplished the great religious reform described in 2 Kings and in 2 Chronicles, when profoundly religious people both in the kingdom of Judea and in the kingdom of Israel are experiencing years of real consolation. It is strange that in Jeremiah we find no mention of those extraordinary events—the rediscovery of Deuteronomy, of the Book of the Law, the renewal of the cult (cf. 2 Kgs 22–23)—which had been the glory of Josiah, one of the greatest kings after David.

However, a rather probable exegetical hypothesis believes that Jeremiah did participate in the euphoria of those years: the northern enemy, Assyria, had defaulted, and the king was reconquering Samaria and Galilee, which had already been occupied for a century.

In order to understand the prophet's joy and hope, we can recall the profound enthusiasm experienced for the event of Vatican II, for the promise of a total renewal of the Church and of society.

Jeremiah sees in the events that are occurring the possibility, the hope that the kingdom of the north may exist again and the deportees come back; it is with this meaning that we must read his words in chapter 31, verses 5-6.

Again you shall plant vineyards
on the mountains of Samaria:
the planters shall plant,
and shall enjoy the fruit.
For there shall be a day when
sentinels will call
in the hill country of Ephraim:
"Come, let us go up to Zion,
to the LORD our God."

Therefore, the pilgrims will return to the holy city from Samaria, separated long ago from Jerusalem and whose inhabitants had been deported to Assyria. In these verses there is perhaps a first prophecy regarding Israel, namely, the kingdom of the north, a first prophecy of that one and only kingdom that had characterized the temples of David.

In brief then, the first draft of chapters 30–31 seems to refer to the reign of Josiah, and hope springs anew in Jeremiah's soul; the Lord forms him through moments of joy and of realizing the success of the religious and political reform.

b) The second period is that of the defeats: the prophecy does not come true and all hopes, both short- and medium-term, vanish in 609 with the death of Josiah, killed by Egypt's pharaoh, and shortly after with the decline of religious feeling, with the rebirth of idolatry in Joachim's reign, and with the imminent threats of Babylonia coming forward.

Jeremiah begins a time of discouragement and bewilderment; how is it that the word of the Lord lied? Why did the prophecy on the northern kingdom not come true? Why did the moral and religious reform of the good king not succeed, and the arms of Israel not win? What was the Lord attempting to say? In 598 B.C., at the time of the fall of Jerusalem, everything seems lost.

It is then that Jeremiah's hope becomes purer and deeper. He sees nothing else besides the fulfillment of his prophecies of misfortune, but he has the courage to believe that their fulfillment guarantees that God's loyalty will come through also for the words of consolation, for the prophecies of hope. God will surely keep his promises, although in a way difficult to explain in human terms.

c) The true season of hope starts with maturation, pain, and suffering. What Jeremiah proclaims through God's command requires complete trust and abandonment: it is a word to be believed, not to be pragmatically verified.

His cry becomes a gospel in the most authentic sense of the word, an invitation to believe: convert and believe in the gospel, not because of what you see, but through faith alone.

Furthermore, Jeremiah's prophecies not only touch the northern kingdom; by now they also reach to the southern kingdom, namely, Judea, to indicate the oneness of the people. It is the moment of enlarging the horizons, of opening to universal dimensions.

Today as well, we hear these oracles resounding precisely because of the prophet's suffering, of his perseverance despite the pain of the damage that had destroyed all the historical hopes of Jerusalem and Israel.

Therefore, the pages of chapters 30–31 are rewritten in a cosmic perspective (according to the exegetical hypothesis previously mentioned): "Thus says the LORD, the God of Israel: Write in a book all the words that I have spoken to you. For the days are surely coming, says the LORD, when I will restore the fortunes of my people, Israel and Judah, says the LORD . . ." (30:2-3), where "Judah" represents the second moment of the prophet's reflection. And in Jeremiah 31:31: "The days are surely coming, says the LORD, when I will make a new covenant with the house of Israel and the house of Judah."

Hence, the fact that in 31:33 it is written: "This is the covenant that I will make with the house of Israel . . . ," would mean that it is a residue of an initial and restricted oracle and only later in a second period extended to all with the announcement of an internal pact ("for they shall all know me"— v. 34). The novelty will involve the whole people and will not so much consist in external changes typical of Josiah's reform but rather in interior changes of the heart. Verse 34 possibly expresses a certain criticism of the king who had presumed he would instill new life in the religious spirit by simply honoring the letter of the Law; but this Law, says Jeremiah, will never be observed if it is not written by God in the hearts of mankind.

The Lord has, therefore, formed his prophet by making him follow a path of disappointment and obscurity to purify his faith, and has brought him to a spiritual height that challenges us closely and expresses the horizons of our personal hope.

Hence, Jeremiah's gospel takes on its definite messianic relevance and is ready to be assumed by future generations, by the very word of Jesus ("This is the cup of the new covenant"—(Luke 22:20) by Paul the apostle ("God has made us competent to be ministers of a new covenant"—2 Cor 3:6), and by the author of the Letter to the Hebrews.

4. Our Ministry of Consolation

After reflecting on the origin of the "book of consolation," and stressing that it comes from great suffering and bitterness experienced in the faith, we want to answer the last question: How are words of real consolation born in us, words that give people courage, that stimulate them to live the interiority of the gospel message?

We know from experience that normally such words come to our lips from a deeply experienced spiritual path and for this reason truly touch the heart. We can reflect, for example, on the story of Paul narrated in the Acts of the Apostles and in his letters. He has arrived at the great cosmic and theological visions of the letters to the Ephesians, to the Philippians, and to the Colossians after many humiliations and many trials.

a) His very first stage is typical of a neophyte preacher, rich with enthusiasm: "Saul became increasingly more powerful and confounded the Jews who lived in Damascus by proving that Jesus was the Messiah" (Acts 9:22).

b) He must, however, flee from Damascus almost immediately because his enthusiasm is obstructed by his enemies' traps, as well as by the fears of the community of his confreres in faith, who sense he is ill at ease, and who fear that in Jerusalem he may create unrest and division. Exiled for many years, marginalized by his intimates, he is then not utilized, reduced to silence, and suffers because he is unable to resign himself to having been set aside.

c) Barnabas goes to look for him at Tarsus in Cilicia and makes him preach again in Antioch. He has not yet fully appropriated the gospel, and even if he peacefully integrates into the Church, he repeats the words of the Kerygma with precision, just as they were given to him. Other experiences and trials however await him, making him shift from an eminently eschatological form of preaching (see letters to the Thessalonians) to a type of homiletics at first polemic and doctrinal on salvation in the here and now (see letters to the Galatians and to the Romans).

d) Finally, through the maturation suffered and experienced in Jerusalem for the conflict of the first council, the persecutions, the enchainment in prison, and the ensuing move to Rome, where he will be judged, he reaches the magnificent, cosmic vision of the letters to the Ephesians and to the Colossians.

Certainly Paul's message—which continues to shake our consciousness even after two thousand years—would not have reached such profound and extensive maturation if the Lord had not placed the evangelist on a path of hard suffering, external and internal disappointments, and very painful events. In this way he could elaborate his gospel. But, just like Jeremiah, he has always been faithful to the voice that had called him on the way to Damascus; he has, in fact, always let hope germinate beneath the trials and mystery of God's silence.

In rethinking our history, our vocation, our lives, each one of us can ask: What has been the meaning of the trials I have experienced? Why did the Lord allow them or Why does he continue to allow them?

I believe that we will truly have discovered the dynamism of God's mystery if we will be enlightened and brave enough to answer that God has allowed such trials precisely to make us ministers of consolation, to make us able to give words of consolation to others.

God, in fact, wishes to make us a chosen instrument of consolation of his people, of a desolate city; he wants us ministers of a new covenant much more than we ourselves wish to be. He does not spare us obscurity nor suffering to fulfill his will, so that the word can be pure, incisive, and convincing.

We ask the Lord, through intercession of the prophet Jeremiah, to let us be formed like clay in the hands of the wise potter, the divine potter who forms in us the word of consolation.

HOMILY

Feast of the Dedication of the Basilica of St. Mary Major

The Ark of the New Covenant

Chapter 21 of the Revelation

The Council of Ephesus (A.D. 431), proclaiming "Mary, the Mother of God," has left in the Church of Rome the visible sign of the Basilica of St. Mary Major, whose dedication we celebrate today. (In the Ambrosian liturgy it remains significant as one of the oldest celebrations of Christianity—"Mary, Mother of God"— celebrated the Sunday before Christmas.)

In this Marian Mass I would like to reflect with you on the first reading, taken from chapter 21 of Revelation:

> Then I saw a new heaven and a new earth; for the first heaven and the first earth had passed away, and the sea was no more. And I saw the holy city, the new Jerusalem, coming down out of heaven from God, prepared as a bride adorned for her husband. And I heard a loud voice from the throne saying,
>
> > "See, the home of God is among mortals,
> > He will dwell with them as their God;
> > they will be his peoples,
> > and God himself will be with them;
> > he will wipe every tear from their eyes.
> > Death will be no more;
> > mourning and crying and pain will be no more,
> > for the first things have passed away."
>
> And the one who was seated on the throne said, "See, I am making all things new." Also he said, "Write this, for these words are trustworthy and true" (Rev 21:1-5).

The Three Prophecies

Chapter 21 of Revelation is also the last word of the New Testament and is of great consolation for all those who weep and suffer.

1. The first part of the oracle is especially meaningful: "See the home of God is among mortals. He will dwell with them as their God. They will be his people."

These are words taken from the prophet Ezekiel, from chapter 37, which corresponds in its content with chapter 31 of Jeremiah, on which we have already meditated.

We certainly recall an episode in Ezekiel 37, the one of the dry bones that the Lord revives by infusing them with the power of the Spirit coming from the four winds. In verse 27 we read: "My dwelling place shall be with them; and I will be their God, and they shall be my people."

With this symbol of a people being reborn, another prophecy of hope and consolation comes to mind, again from Ezekiel: "I will put my spirit within you, and make you follow my statutes and be careful to observe my ordinances . . . and you shall be my people and I will be your God. . . . I will sprinkle clean water upon you, and you shall be clean from all your uncleannesses" (Ezek 36:27-28, 25). "I will put my spirit within you" is almost the identical corresponding verse to Jeremiah 31:33: "I will put my law within them, and I will write it on their hearts."

These are two important passages that Paul will take up again to indicate that the New Testament is the temple of the Spirit.

2. In the second part of the oracle—"and he will be God-with-them"—the visionary of the Apocalypse picks up Isaiah 7:4: "And the virgin will conceive and give birth to a son and he will be called Emmanuel." And when the evangelist Matthew will want to explain who Jesus is, he will recall just this Isaian prophecy of the Emmanuel (see Matt 1:23).

3. Even the third part of the oracle: "He will wipe every tear from their eyes. Death will be no more; mourning and crying

and pain will be no more, for the first things have passed away," makes reference to Isaiah, who prophesies the great messianic banquet on the holy mountain, when God will remove the black cloth of mourning and will dry every tear (25:8).

Therefore, in recalling the Old Testament, the excerpt from Revelation sends the theme, the promise of hope, of comfort, of consolation to all Christian generations, including our own.

Mary, Ark of the Covenant

If we contemplate the figure of Mary, we realize that it beautifully expresses the content of the oracle.

She is the temple of the Lord, the sanctuary of the new covenant: it is through her that we enter into a stable covenant with God; it is the *foederis arca*, the sign of God-with-us. In fact, in Mary, the communion of God with humanity is fully realized, and for this reason we invoke her as the consoler of the afflicted, of those who weep.

I would, therefore, like to invite you to make a symbolic visit to some Marian shrine. When I was in Rome, for instance, I used to often visit the sanctuary of Divine Love; as I prayed, I would watch the people passing in front of the Virgin saying to myself: How many tears and suffering are placed at the feet of Mary that she then relieves in her maternal way. And so, thinking of others, I realized that my small problems and difficulties were really not important. As I left the sanctuary I would then feel moved to console the suffering of the people, of families, of mothers, fathers, spouses, the suffering of the young and the unemployed, of the aged who are alone and abandoned. I knew that Mary dried all their tears, and I wanted in some way to take part in her mission.

> O Mary, teach us to dry the tears of the women and men of our earth, of our diocese; teach us not to pay too much attention to our problems, but to behave as you do, listening to the sufferings and pain of everyone; teach us to console all those who wait for a word of comfort and hope.

11.

Pastoral Love

Pastoral Love and the Image of Rachel

Since Vatican Council II and in all Church documents up to the encyclical *Pastores dabo vobis*, "pastoral love" is a concise concept that wants to clarify the overall duties of the pastor. In reality it is simply love as a gift of God, infused in all hearts by the Holy Spirit, the participation of humankind in the love of God but directed toward a particular people, lavished on a part of the fold of the Lord.

The theme of pastoral love or charity is one that in a certain sense summarizes the preceding meditations, because it is the same theme that God has inspired in the prophets and in Jeremiah for his people; it is the love that Jesus inspires in us for the people entrusted to us and which sanctifies us. In fact, we are sanctified, as are all Christians, through love, which is the bond of perfection.

If Jeremiah has suffered so much, wept, preached, cried out, albeit with the feeling of crying out in vain, he did so because he was moved by this pastoral love, and it seems appropriate, then, to conclude our exercises reflecting on such a theme.

The referential text contains the oracle on Rachel weeping for her children (Jer 31:15-16), in which we can glimpse the charity of the pastor for those he loves, the loving charity of Mother Church for her children. This oracle is the only one quoted explicitly as being Jeremiah's by the New Testament, in the story of the childhood of Jesus. When speaking of the massacre of the innocents, Matthew writes, "Then was fulfilled what had been spoken through the prophet Jeremiah: "A voice was heard in Ramah, wailing and loud lamentation, Rachel weeping for her children. She refused to be consoled because they are no more" (Matt 2:17-18).

Many other texts of Jeremiah are cited, however, without explicit mention (for instance, Jeremiah 31 in Hebrews 8).

It is true that Matthew, telling the story of Judas' thirty coins with which the high priests bought the field of the potter, comments: "Then was fulfilled what had been spoken through the prophet Jeremiah, 'And they took the thirty pieces of silver, the price of the one on whom a price had been set, on whom some of the people of Israel had set a price, and they gave them for the potter's field, as the Lord commanded me'" (Matt 27:9-10). But we know that the clarification of the thirty denarii belongs instead to the prophet Zechariah (see Zech 11).

Therefore, I think it is interesting to reflect on the only quote expressed by Jeremiah, also to understand how it teaches us to read the New Testament, and how it introduces us to the free and open reading of Holy Scripture that was characteristic of the Fathers of the Church.

So we will observe a few texts of the Fathers, to then conclude with a question regarding our pastoral love: In what way should we pray for the city? How does pastoral love work in the intercession for the people of large cities?

Lectio of Jeremiah 31:15-17: Lamentation and Hope

The oracle is very brief:

> Thus says the LORD:
> A voice is heard in Ramah,
>   lamentation and bitter weeping.
> Rachel is weeping for her children;
>   she refuses to be comforted for her children,
>   because they are no more.
> Thus says the LORD:

Keep your voice from weeping,
　　and your eyes from tears;
　for there is a reward for your work,
　　says the LORD:
　　they shall come back from the land of the enemy;
　there is hope for your future, says the LORD:
　　your children shall come back to their own country
　　(Jer 31:15-17).

The passage contains two parts: the first part is one of lamentation, pain, and mourning, the second of hope. It therefore summarizes well the Book of Jeremiah: suffering and hope, tears, and the opening of the heart.

Twice Jeremiah writes "Thus says the LORD," and twice he writes "says the LORD"), thus underlining the importance attributed by the prophet to the image of Rachel emerging almost out of the shadows.

1. Verse 15 expresses suffering in different forms: a shout, a lament, a bitter, inconsolable weeping. A suffering by now definite, as that of a widowed mother crying because her son will never return, a suffering that human words fail to describe.

And we hear it from Ramah. We recall here a passage of Jeremiah on which we have already dwelled:

> The word that came to Jeremiah from the LORD after Nebuzaradan the captain of the guard had let him go from Ramah, when he took him bound in fetters along with all the captives of Jerusalem and Judah, who were being exiled to Babylon (40:1).

Ramah is the place of weeping. We also know that Nebuzaradan will free the prophet, who should therefore experience a moment of joy; but in fact he sees his brothers in chains and deported to the enemy city, and he bursts into tears for that seemingly irrevocable exile. It is from Ramah itself that the caravan headed for Babylonia is formed.

　—It is Rachel who cries, ancient mother of the patriarchs, whose tomb is located near Ramah: Jeremiah sees her as a symbol of the Jewish people, as the woman who sees her sons' deportation and weeps.

This image brings immediately to mind the painful reality of a persecuted people who still today weeps for its suffering, praying in front of the so-called "wailing wall," the west wall of the temple.

Rachel represents this people as a mother who cannot be consoled because there is no hope left for her children. They are physically alive, of course, but to be in exile, out of the city, out of one's own country is the same as entering death, as being abandoned by the Lord.

2. The second part of the oracle, which corresponds point by point to the first, follows the very incisive description of verse 15: "Keep your voice from weeping and your eyes from tears; for there is a reward for your work; they shall come back from the land of the enemy" (v. 16).

The great crying, the many tears, must cease because you will be rewarded for your sufferings: "There is hope for your future, your children shall come back to their own country" (v. 17).

Those words appear to be insane, since they are pronounced just as the long file of deportees heads out to Babylonia; yet, projected through the centuries, in the future of God, they form the hope of resurrection of a whole people. It is truly an oracle of extraordinary strength, holding within itself that pain and joy typical of Jeremiah's message. By using symbols already mentioned, we could say: The broken jug can be miraculously repaired, the rotten loincloth can also be miraculously brought back to its early splendor, the ill-formed vase can be rebuilt.

Contemplating the tears of his people, Jeremiah announces a marvelous hope for the future.

3. Let us now attempt to capture the rich resonance of the New Testament text, to understand how it is being reread in its themes of crying, suffering, pain for its people, and hope.

Matthew 2:17-18 is based on the assonance of the same name between the historic city of Ramah, north of Jerusalem, and a site close to Bethlehem. Thus the evangelist transfers the prophecy, applying it to the crying of the mothers of Bethlehem for their children killed by King Herod's command. He doesn't go into depth on the theological connection, nor does he relate the joyous part of the oracle, but it can be considered implicit; if the mothers bear their suffering for Jesus, for them, too, there will surely be a joy, a reward. Every year, on the feast of the Holy Innocents, the Church celebrates the glory of this suffering, the opening to hope found in suffering, so we should therefore not exclude such an opening in the story of Matthew referring to Jeremiah.

Other New Testament passages recall the oracle of the prophet on weeping and hope. Out of many episodes to consider, I remember a particularly significant one: the crying of Mary Magdalene for the son of her people who died, for that Son of Israel who represented hope and is no longer.

> But Mary stood weeping outside the tomb. As she wept, she bent over to look into the tomb; and she saw two angels in white, sitting where the body of Jesus had been lying, one at the head and the other at the feet. They said to her: "Woman, why are you weeping" (John 20:11).

In the passage, the weeping of Mary is greatly underscored; she is the new Rachel who bemoans the end of hope for her people, the woman of whom the disciples of Emmaus will speak: "But we had hoped that he was the one to redeem Israel. Yes, and besides all this, it is now the third day since these things took place" (Luke 24:21).

We find the same weeping for an apparently lost hope in the sisters of Lazarus, especially in Mary:

> When Mary came where Jesus was and saw him, she knelt at his feet and said to him, "Lord, if you had been here, my brother would not have died." When Jesus saw her weeping, and the Jews who came with her also weeping, he was greatly disturbed

in spirit and deeply moved. He said, "Where have you laid him?" They said to him, "Lord, come and see" (John 11:32-35).

And here we also see that Jesus takes upon himself the weeping of the people, he embodies pastoral love, feels the same depth of despair in Rachel's crying, and begins to weep for a son of his people that symbolizes the death of sin, the condition of death of humanity. He is moved because pastoral love means taking on the bitter and painful destiny of the women and men of this earth, just as Jeremiah was moved by the bitter and painful fate of Jerusalem.

On the background of the scene in which Jesus becomes involved with the suffering of his friends, of the people he loves, I wish also to emphasize that his pastoral love expresses itself even more directly in Luke 19:41:

> As he came near and saw the city, he wept over it, saying, "If you, even you, had only recognized on this day the things that make for peace! But now they are hidden from your eyes."

Just as Rachel weeps upon those who have not heard the word of God and are now going into exile, as Mary, Lazarus' sister, weeps on the hope that has been lost, in the same way Jesus enters into the suffering of the people who fail to see the moment of salvation.

Pastoral love takes part in the mercy and suffering of Jesus for his people, which lead him to cry for Lazarus and for the city; he takes part in the tears of Rachel and of Mary Magdalene, while still taking into account the second part of Jeremiah's oracle, the announcement that tears will be wiped away.

In this regard, we have the key words of the Beatitudes: "Blessed are you who weep now, for you will laugh" (Luke 6:21). We can apply this to pastoral love: Blessed are those who know how to weep for the sufferings of their people, for their sins, because this is the way to enter into harmony with the mercy of Jesus and to contemplate the hope of the future. We should not, therefore, hide all the suffering, faithlessness, and negligence, but rather make them ours, enter into them by crying while all along glimpsing a future of hope: "Blessed are those who mourn, for they will be comforted" (Matt 5:4). I will take a last passage from the Book of Revelation: "[God] will wipe every tear from their eyes" (21:4). These are the tears for physical death, especially those that are shed for ignoring God, for sins, and for all forms of humanity's pain.

The oracle of Jeremiah 31:15-17 resonates, therefore, in the New Testament, according to various melodies.

Meditatio: How to Read Sacred Scripture

In the moment of the meditation, I invite you to reflect on three paths.

How Is One to Read the Old Testament in the New Testament?

We are a part of a rational, technical, logical, and scientific society, and are therefore rightly concerned about approaching the Scriptures on a scientific basis. I, too, have undertaken a solid, objective, serious reading that is rooted in the text and does not invent meanings.

However, once the text has been seriously and objectively established, we must learn to apply a certain freedom, such as is found in the New Testament. Matthew, for example, freely uses parts of the oracle of Jeremiah, who cries about the deportees, in order to apply it to a situation he is experiencing.

We therefore have the right and the duty to rethink our current sufferings, our difficulties, and pastoral problems along the words of Jeremiah. In fact, they are not only transmitted so that we can retrace their historic context, but so that these words can help us to interpret the present. This is the freedom with which the New Testament reads the Old, and the freedom with which the Church reads Scripture. And our informal, familiar use of the Bible is very important, though it depends on us; if Scripture is foreign to us, we approach it fearfully, but if we know it and consider it as a precious good, we then use it with freedom, namely, in a familiar way.

All the pages of the Old Testament can, therefore, help us to understand ourselves, to read our story and the stages of our path freely. Then the threats, the laments, and the invectives of Jeremiah are valid for each historic suffering of the Church and of society; and the consolations of Jeremiah are alive to assuage each historic weeping of the Church and of society.

The pages of the prophet are applicable to our pain and to that of our loved ones, to the suffering of such a large part of humanity, to the conflicts between nations and people, to the suffering of all the outcasts and the poor, to the pain of the cities at war, to the many tears we try to share in order to accompany all the women and men on earth. I am more and more convinced that to help the poor, for example, one has to suffer with them, understand and love them; pastoral love does not help us meet others if we remain above them or distant, but opens our hearts to a deep empathy and sensitivity that places us next to Rachel crying for her children's hunger, for the problems and suffering of daily life.

Scripture in the Fathers

Even the Church Fathers read Scripture with an interpretive freedom that allows them to extend pastoral love to all the situations of their times. Among many examples, I am choosing a beautiful one from St. Ambrose who, in the "Treatise on Penance," applies to himself and to others the weeping of Jesus for Lazarus, narrated in John's gospel (John 11:35).

First of all he writes: "Jesus cries for me." (He puts himself in the place of Lazarus.)

> Please deign, O Lord, to come to this my tomb, to wash me with your tears because my parched, dry eyes do not contain enough to wash away my sins. If you will cry with me, I will be saved; if I am worthy of your tears, I will wash away the stench of all my sins. If I am worthy that you cry a few instants for me, you will call me from my bodily tomb and say: Come forth!, so that my thoughts do not stay in the restricted space of this body,

but come out to meet Christ and live in the light, so that I will not think of works of darkness, but of works of light.

Ambrose relives the mystery of his penance, of his rebirth, of his calling to grace in the tears of Jesus for Lazarus. And, at a certain point, he relives the same mystery of pastoral life, of episcopal ordination and, continuing his prayer exclaims: "Maintain your grace, Lord, protect the gift you have given me despite my refusals." (He did not, in fact, wish to become bishop.) "Since I have faced some burdens for your Holy Church, please continue those results. Do not allow him, whom you called to the episcopacy when he was lost, to become lost now that he is bishop *(De Penitentia,* P.L. 16: Lib. II, 8:71-73; *Sancti Ambrosii Episcopi Mediolanensis Opera).*

Ambrose, after having freely taken on himself Jesus' tears for Lazarus, which he expressed in a public sermon where he declares himself first of all a sinner, then continues with his participation in Jesus' tears for others, in pastoral love for the people. "Allow me to be able to share with intimate participation the pain of sinners." This, in fact, is the highest virtue, because it is written:

> . . . you should not have rejoiced
>   over the people of Judah
>   on the day of their ruin;
> you should not have boasted
>   on the day of distress (Obad 12).

"In fact, every time the sin of a fallen one is in question, allow me to feel compassion for that person and not to reproach him with disdain, but rather to moan and cry, so that while I cry over another I cry over myself" (ibid.).

Let us capture in these words the height of pastoral love typical of the person who considers the other as himself, of the one who reads in the suffering and sins of another his own sufferings and sins because he has come to be one with those he loves and who are entrusted to his ministry.

How Is One to Pray for the City in the Spirit of Jeremiah?

The authors of the New Testament and the Fathers of the Church help us to reflect on ourselves and on the way we become involved in the paths of those persons whom the Lord places on our way.

At times, when praying in the evening in the chapel in front of the Blessed Sacrament or in my room, I think painfully of the many sins committed at night in a large city: episodes of violence, drugs, prostitution, crimes, thefts, adultery, betrayals, and both social and political swindles. Faced with such continuous and numerous sins in the city, we could be tempted to bring very severe judgments, haughty reproaches, merciless criticisms, as if following the tendencies of the press and public opinion. But our feeling of being morally superior is malicious and makes us victims of that type of self-justification that the apostle Paul so harshly criticized.

Jeremiah, Jesus, and the saints never had such an attitude contrary to gospel principles: they have instead cried for the suffering and the sins of the city as if they were their own. Pastoral love shows itself through hatred of evil; this form of charity makes us all feel such a deep empathy for the person doing the evil that we are in pain for him, we stay close to his side, invoking the miracle of God, in the hope that Christ Jesus has already conquered all the evils of humanity.

When in the evening I think of the sins of my city, (which touch me directly as pastor because they are all infidelities to the gospel I preach) after having felt almost physically upon me the weight of these faults, errors, ignorance (errors not always intentional, but destructive for the human being), I then feel serene in the light of this certitude.

I tell myself, in fact, that a drop of Jesus' blood washes away every horrible thing, every crime, every form of violence because everything has already been carried on the cross, is already forgiven; he calls his children home, the women and men of every era and every nation, he calls them to return from exile, to live anew, and Jeremiah's positive oracle flows over them. The Lord does not fear any type of separation and gives life to all of humanity.

At the end of the exercises, we then return to our ministry comforted by the mercy of the heart of Christ, by the contemplation of the crucifix that cries out: "Father, forgive them; for they do not know what they are doing" (Luke 23:34), knowing that forgiveness is first of all for us, for each of us, that it involves everyone, and takes us into the embrace of the risen one.

The Lord wants to inspire in us who are pastors of a confused and suffering city the attitude of one who has a deep sense of sin, of fault, of lack of knowledge of God, of the injustices being plotted in the world, but at the same time has the expression of Jesus, a glance full of hope and mercy. Let us pray for each other, in the desire that this be truly the daily expression of our pastoral love, so as to remain confident and at peace even in a corrupt, complex, and confused society such as ours.

HOMILY

Feast of the Lord's Transfiguration

Transfigured from Glory to Glory

A Central and Condensed Mystery

We wish to remember first of all the fifteenth anniversary of the death of Paul VI, August 6, 1978, on the feast of the mystery of the Transfiguration that he loved so much.

It is a central mystery of the gospel, and it also occupies a central spot in the stories of the evangelists: it is placed, in fact, just after Peter's confession, among the key episodes marking the passage from the first to the second part of the ministry of Jesus. In this image of Christ transfigured (Mark 9:2-10; Luke 9:28-36; Matt 17:1-8) we read a synthesis between the Old and New Testaments: Moses who represents the law, Elijah, who represents the prophets and Jesus. The Old and New Testaments are composed as a whole because Jesus realizes the unity of the whole plan of God.

It is, furthermore, a synthesis between humiliation and glory. He who is transfigured is the humble Jesus of public life who seemed just a man like other men, while he is, in fact, the Son in whom the light of the Father shines.

Synthesis between humiliation and glory, and synthesis between death and resurrection; according to Luke's story, the words exchanged between Elijah, Moses, and Jesus refer to the exodus, death, and glorification of Jesus that would have taken place in Jerusalem.

And again, it is a synthesis between humanity and divinity. The voice says: See that this man is my beloved Son, that the humble Jesus is the Son of God.

A Prophetic Mystery

Yet the transfiguration is also a prophetic mystery because it both anticipates the resurrection of Christ and announces what we all will become if we follow Christ.

The Greek Church, particularly Byzantine Orthodox monasticism, sees in the mystery the path to transfiguration characteristic of an ascetic, eremitic, and mystical life, a path of transfiguring humanity into divinity, of elevation of all humanity into the glory of Jesus.

With this intuition on the other hand, the ascetic and mystical practices of Greek monasticism simply recapture the works of St. Paul where he explains the New Covenant: "And all of us, with unveiled faces, seeing the glory of the Lord as though reflected in a mirror, are being transformed into the same image from one degree of glory to another; for this comes from the Lord, the Spirit" (2 Cor 3:18).

Christian life is a transfiguration, from one glory to another, in the working of the Spirit and in fixing one's gaze on the face of Jesus.

Conclusion of the Exercises

Our spiritual exercises, which are brought to a close with the Eucharist, have really aimed at helping us to transform our lives. As we recognize ourselves to be weak and poor, in need of constant purification, a humble voice such as that of Jeremiah's, we have felt that God's will calls us to become his voice, the word of the Lord for the people entrusted to us; it calls us to a path of personal transfiguration, enlightened as we are by the glory that shines in the face of Christ and in the word of God. It is a glory that changes as we gradually assimilate this word with the *lectio divina* and with the Eucharist; it is the Christian path, our path, and that of our people. We become transfigured along with the others: not "I" but "we."

I seem to be capturing the final message for each one of you, bishops and presbyters of the churches of Venezuela: Transfigure this people. Transform its tears, its burdens, its suffering, its faith, in joy and in rest, in justice and in truth. Each of you transfigures the people by transfiguring yourself.

The Church here and elsewhere, has the great responsibility and task to surround the people with the glory of Jesus, starting from the faith, the simplicity, and the human truths that people possess.

And I thank the Lord for the gift of having lived these days, making me a participant in some way in the commitment you are assuming, allowing me to enjoy your friendship, to be enriched by your faith, and to appreciate the extremely warm hospitality of your people that from one glory to another is being transfigured in the image of Jesus.